Everyday
English

Everyday
English

{ How to Say What You Mean
and Write Everything Right }

Patrick Scrivenor

Reader's
Digest

The Reader's Digest Association, Inc.
New York, NY / Montreal

A READER'S DIGEST BOOK

FOR READER'S DIGEST
U.S. Editor: Barbara Booth
Consulting Editor: Stephanie Schwartz
Copy Editor: Gesina Phillips
Manager, English Book Editorial, Reader's Digest Canada: Pamela Johnson
Designer: Jennifer Tokarski
Managing Editor: Lorraine Burton
Senior Art Director: George McKeon
Associate Publisher, Trade Publishing: Rosanne McManus
President and Publisher, Trade Publishing: Harold Clarke
Editor-in-Chief, North America: Liz Vaccariello
President, North America: Dan Lagani
President and CEO, Reader's Digest Association, Inc.: Robert E. Guth

Illustrations by Andrew Pinder

Library of Congress Cataloging-in-Publication Data
Scrivenor, Patrick, 1943-
 Everyday English : how to say what you mean and write everything right /
Patrick Scrivenor.
    p. cm.
 Includes index.
 ISBN 978-1-60652-482-4 -- ISBN 978-1-60652-484-8 (adobe) -- ISBN 978-1-
60652-483-1 (e pub)
1. English language--Grammar. 2. English language--Spoken English. I. Title.
PE1112.S378 2012
 428.2--dc23

                                    2011053114

We are committed to both the quality of our products and the service we provide
to our customers. We value your comments, so please feel free to contact us.

        The Reader's Digest Association, Inc.
        Adult Trade Publishing
        44 South Broadway, White Plains, NY 10601

For more Reader's Digest products and information, visit our website:
        www.rd.com (in the United States)
        www.readersdigest.ca (in Canada)

Printed in the United States

1 3 5 7 9 10 8 6 4 2

"To be fair, English is full of booby traps for the unwary. . . . Any language where the unassuming word *fly* signifies an annoying insect, a means of travel, and a critical part of a gentleman's apparel is clearly asking to be mangled."

—Bill Bryson, *Mother Tongue*

Contents

Clear Usage 123

Pitfalls and Confusions 137

Introduction

How much grammar can you remember? Do you know the difference between a phrase and a clause? Is it second nature never to use a preposition at the end of a sentence? Are you clear on the distinction between *will* and *shall*?

This book will take you back to the classroom and reacquaint you with all the stuff you might have once seen scrawled across the blackboard. I have tried to retain the traditional terms of grammar that you would have heard at school. I have had to feel my way to some extent with this, since how you were taught English grammar depends to some extent on *where* you attended school and how *long* ago. But we are concerned here only with how to use vocabulary, grammar, punctuation, and spelling to write clear, concise English.

There are many varieties of English. Which variety were you taught at school? The likelihood is that you were taught standard written English—the formal version of English taught both to mother-tongue English speakers and to people learning English as a second language. There are even different varieties of standard English, British and

American being the two main ones. But their similarities far outweigh their differences, and standard English is well on its way to becoming an international language.

How can so many varieties of English exist? Languages are continually evolving, and what look like set rules are constantly modified or even abandoned. It can be hard to determine what is correct and what incorrect. In fact, languages actually predate their rules. They are usually in existence, and freely spoken, long before they are written and long before anyone starts to systematize their rules. They rarely have rules that have been thought out logically in advance. Even languages that developed in a period of literacy, such as modern English, evolved through being used.

All the same, in the classroom we were taught the difference between formal English and colloquial English. We were taught to obey certain rules of grammar, vocabulary, and spelling, and these constitute our understanding of what is good English. To be a strong communicator, it helps to know these rules—even if you are going to break them.

—*Patrick Scrivenor*

Parts of Speech

Words are formed using letters. The five vowels and twenty-one consonants in the alphabet express sounds made by the human vocal cords, tongue, and mouth. Together or singly, these sounds make words. The parts of speech classify words by what they do. So nouns name people, places, and things; verbs express action; adjectives modify nouns; adverbs modify verbs; pronouns stand in for nouns; and so on.

Of course, it sounds so much easier than it actually is. Grammarians throughout the ages have delighted in splitting hairs and making distinctions. Even after ditching the most troublesome, there are still many variants within all the parts of speech.

Here's the simplest introduction to understanding the parts of speech and their roles within a sentence.

Nouns

Name It and Shame It?

Things are named by **common nouns**. One example is the concrete noun, which names something that has a physical existence:

house   *rock* ✓

Another is the abstract noun, which names something that has no physical existence:

success ✓   *failure*

Naming Names

> *"Every Tom, Dick, and Harry is named John!"*
> **—SAM GOLDWYN, FILM PRODUCER**

Your own names are nouns. In fact, they are **proper nouns,** which name a specific person, place, or thing:

Jessica Simpson ✓
George Washington Bridge
Oklahoma

The first letter of a proper noun is capitalized. Proper nouns that refer to events are often preceded by *the*:

the Industrial Revolution ✓
the Great Depression

Titles of persons are capitalized when followed by their name; they are lowercased when standing alone:

President Lincoln; the president
Queen Elizabeth; the queen

It is not always easy to distinguish proper nouns from other nouns. For instance, the names of birds or flowers refer to a single "thing," but unless they are specific, they are lowercased:

sparrow; Eurasian Tree Sparrow
tulip; Darwin Hybrid Tulip

Common Sense

Some proper nouns have become common nouns through use. These are usually things named after their inventor or manufacturer. *Kleenex* (when referring to a tissue) and *Xerox* (when referring to a photocopy) are two well-known examples. Xerox has even taken on use as a verb! Much longer-standing examples, which are no longer capped in the dictionary, are *leotard,* after Jules Léotard, a nineteenth-century 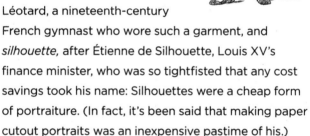 French gymnast who wore such a garment, and *silhouette,* after Étienne de Silhouette, Louis XV's finance minister, who was so tightfisted that any cost savings took his name: Silhouettes were a cheap form of portraiture. (In fact, it's been said that making paper cutout portraits was an inexpensive pastime of his.)

Two for the Price of One

Compound nouns are formed when words are tacked together to form a single term. Sometimes the words are separate:

cat burglar ✓
mountain pass
shoe box

Occasionally they are hyphenated:

bull's-eye
son-in-law
bird-watcher

And many times they are run together as one word:

girlfriend   *workforce*
mailman   *database*

There are few hard-and-fast rules as to which words should be hyphenated or open and which run together to form one word. But one rule is to always use a hyphen when a word would be confusing without one: for example, *re-create*. Usage, as always, plays a part in deciding which to do. With time some hyphenated compounds dropped their hyphens to become one word, such as *week-end* and b*aby-sitter*. When in doubt, check a dictionary.

Hyphen Help

Nouns that begin with *self, all,* or *ex* are always hyphenated:

self-doubt, all-powerful, ex-husband

Nouns You Can Count On

Some nouns refer to things that can be counted:

cars   *cows*
posts   *tiles*

Others name things that can be quantified only generally:

distance   *gas*
intelligence   *water*

If you can ask the question "How many?" you have a **countable noun.** For instance, you can ask, "How many cars?" but you can't ask, "How many distance?" Therefore, "distance" is a noncountable noun.

This distinction enables you to make the difference between the usage of *fewer* and *less*. *Fewer* is used with countable nouns:

There are fewer cars today.

Less is used with **noncountable nouns:**

There is less traffic today.

All Together Now: Collective Nouns

Collective nouns name a group or a number of people or things:

committee	*family*
herd	*team*

Collective nouns are usually singular, because the collective is thought of as a unit:

The committee <u>was</u> unable to meet.

When adjectives are treated as collective nouns—the needy, the unemployed, the good, the wealthy—they are always plural:

The unemployed <u>are</u> mostly young and homeless.

Strangely, there are a huge number of collective nouns that all mean "group" but are specific to the animal they are referring to:

a covey of grouse	*a flock of birds*
a herd of cattle	*a pod of dolphins*
a sleuth of bears	*an army of ants*

Others are onomatopoeic:

a gaggle of geese
a murmuration of starlings

But many are contrived and used ironically, or as oddities, rather than seriously:

a dependence of daughters
a guzzle of aldermen
an ostentation of peacocks

Nouns from Verbs

A final class of nouns is derived directly from verbs (**verbal nouns**), sometimes with alteration and sometimes using the same word:

arrive/arrival	*destroy/destruction*
attack/attack	*return/return*

In addition, some verb forms, such as **gerunds** and **present participles**—verbs that end in *-ing,* like *jumping* and *swinging* (see page 25)—can be used as nouns.

Three's a Crowd

In English the **plural** is usually formed simply by adding *-s* to the noun:

book/books	*bottle/bottles*
clock/clocks	*light/lights*

However, there are a wide range of English words in which different rules must be applied, such as:

- those that already end in *s*
- those that end in a similar sound, like *x* or *z*
- those that end in *ch* or *s*
- those that end in *y* preceded by a consonant

In the following nouns the plural is formed by adding *-es*, with any *y* becoming *i*:

dress/dresses   *fax/faxes*
waltz/waltzes   *torch/torches*
baby/babies
fish/fishes (but *fish*
is also accepted as a
plural form)

Below are some examples
where *o* endings take *-es*:

potato/potatoes
tomato/tomatoes
hero/heroes

However, here they do not:

disco/discos
solo/solos

It doesn't stop there. Normally, words ending in *f* or *fe* form the plural with -*ves*:

leaf/leaves
wife/wives

And again, there are many exceptions:

belief/beliefs
chief/chiefs
proof/proofs

There are even some cases with *two* acceptable plurals:

hoof/hoofs/hooves
dwarf/dwarfs/dwarves
wharf/wharfs/wharves

Then there are the plurals that obey Greek or Latin rules, foisted on us by our classics-besotted ancestors:

crisis/crises   *criterion/criteria*
millennium/millennia   *phenomenon/phenomena*
terminus/termini

But in some cases you can ignore the classical ending and just tack on -*es* or -*s*:

ignoramus/ignoramuses
referendum/referendums

Sometimes you even have a choice:

cactus/cacti/cactuses
index/indexes/indices

In addition, there are endings that stem from Old English:

ox/oxen
child/children

There are also plurals that are made by changing the vowel sound (a process known as ablaut):

goose/geese
man/men
tooth/teeth

Some nouns have no plural:

dust
furniture
silverware
wheat

Others have *only* a plural form:

pants   *scissors*
shorts   *pliers*

Then there are nouns that appear plural because they have an -s at the end but are usually treated as singular. These include, for example, the names of subjects or disciplines— *ethics, linguistics*—that end in *-ics*. When used strictly to refer to the discipline named, they are singular:

Politics is a disreputable trade.
Physics is the most exacting of the sciences.

When used more generally, they are plural:

His politics are far to the left of center.
The physics of it are highly complex.

And it also includes the names of many diseases, games, and places:

diabetes	*dominoes*	*the Bahamas*
measles	*darts*	*the Balkans*

If you think that's chaotic, be grateful that nouns in the English language do not have cases—variants of the noun (usually variant endings) that do the work of other words. (Pronouns do, however: see page 43.) In a language that is case-encumbered, "government of the people, by the people, and for the people" would be expressed by using different endings for the word "people." Fortunately, English nouns do not have genders, either. It is the absence of case and gender that makes English such a delightfully easy language to learn—until you get to verbs.

Verbs

> *"Verbing weirds language."*
> —BILL WATTERSON, CREATOR OF *CALVIN AND HOBBES*

Verbs *do.* By itself this might not be a helpful definition, but take a look at the following phrases:

I dogs   *You incompetent*
We each other

At present they are meaningless. However, if you add the words "love," "are," and "dislike," they immediately tell you something. Because verbs make things happen, they are at the heart of the sentence. There are, of course, plenty of examples of verbless "sentences," where the verb is absent but understood (see page 66, "Fragments").

But by and large, groups of words without a verb are like a car without an engine—they can't go anywhere.

Verbs differ from other parts of speech. Below are several ways in which the verb "to walk" can be used.

1. Verbs can express tense—past, present, and future:

I walked.   *You walk.*
We will walk.

> **Sentence Strategy**
>
> Lots of people make the simple mistake of using present participles as nouns. In the following sentence, the word "letting" is the present participle, acting as a verbal noun, and should therefore be preceded by the possessive pronoun "his" (see page 48). "Him letting" would be wrong.
>
> *I admire his letting her go.*

2. They can be supported by helping verbs (see page 27):

I have walked four miles.
You are walking from California to Maine.

3. Verbs can become nouns by forming gerunds (see page 27), usually by adding *-ing*:

Walking four miles a day reduces the risk of heart disease.

4. The present participle *walking*, like the gerund, can also act as a noun:

I protested his walking alone.

5. Verbs can take a **subject**—a noun, phrase, or clause—indicating who or what is doing something, as well as an **object**—again a noun, phrase, or clause—indicating to what or to whom it is being done.

Verbs are usually categorized as **transitive** or **intransitive**, but some—**labile** verbs—can be both.

Transitive verbs take a direct object:

I killed Cock Robin.   *You want a good job.*
He seduced her.

The verbs *kill, want,* and *seduce* are true transitive verbs. That is, if you left out the object, the sentence would be incomplete, although it would carry a vague meaning, leaving the reader or the listener wanting the rest of the story. He seduced. . . . Please continue—you've left out the juicy details!

Intransitive verbs take no direct object:

I arrived.   *Time elapsed.*
The lady vanishes.

Labile verbs can be used with an object but also make sense without one:

He smokes a pipe./He smokes.
We sank the Bismarck.*/The*
   Bismarck *sank.*

A Verb Is a Noun Is a Verb: The Gerund

This is a word that strikes terror into anyone who ever studied Latin. But it's really not that bad. It just means the form of the verb that acts as a noun. In the sentence "I enjoy taking long walks," *taking* is a gerund. The entire phrase, "taking long walks," is a noun phrase, and it is the object of the verb *enjoy*. Enjoying yourself yet?

Verbs can also be categorized as either **lexical** or **helping** verbs. Lexical verbs are all those that are not helping verbs, and they function as the main verb of a sentence. Below, *like* is the lexical verb and *would* the helping verb:

I would like to be a concert pianist.

There are 16 helping, or auxiliary, verbs in English. Three are primary auxiliaries, used to compound other verbs: *be, do* and *have*. Thirteen are modal auxiliaries, used to express mood and, in some cases, tense: *can, could, dare, may, might, must, need, ought, shall, should, used, will,* and *would*.

With these exceptions, all verbs are lexical and all verbs can be expressed in the **infinitive** form, in various **conjugations**, in various **tenses**, in one of two **voices**, and in various **moods**.

To Be or Not to Be: The Infinitive

> *"To boldly go where no man has gone before."*
> **—STAR TREK**

More ink has been spilled over this tiny point than over any other grammatical issue. The **infinitive** is the simplest expression of a verb's meaning, unencumbered by tense, mood, or person. In English, to distinguish it from other verb forms, the infinitive is preceded by the participle "to."

Oh, dear. The word "to" is *not* part of the infinitive, although it is used with the infinitive. Because of the influence of Latin—in which it is impossible to divide an infinitive verb—it has been standard in the past to avoid the "split infinitive": the introduction of a modifying word between "to" and the verb, as above in the *Star Trek* preamble. The rule became: Never split an infinitive.

> *"When I split an infinitive, God damn it, I split it*
> *so it will stay split."*
> —SCREENWRITER RAYMOND CHANDLER, COMPLAINING
> TO THE EDITOR OF THE *ATLANTIC MONTHLY* AFTER A
> PROOFREADER HAD ALTERED WHAT CHANDLER HAD
> INTENDED TO BE "BARROOM VERNACULAR"

Many modern grammarians have been at pains to pooh-pooh the split-infinitive rule, claiming that it is illogical and smacks of small-mindedness, that the alternatives can sound artificial, that a split infinitive can plainly mean exactly what it says, as in "Our object is to further improve international relations."

Despite all these excellent reasons, I unhesitatingly recommend: Don't split an infinitive. A split infinitive sounds cumbersome, and it almost always puts the modifying word—"boldly," in the *Star Trek* example—into a place where it has a weak effect. "To go boldly"—puts the emphasis on the "boldly," which is where it should be. There is a general rule of sentence construction in English that each word should go where it belongs, where it has the most effect. A split infinitive usually risks breaking this rule.

But not always. It is possible to construct a sentence in which a split infinitive gives the best reading:

The police installed roadside cameras to secretly film motorists speeding.

In this example the only alternative position for the word *secretly* that gives the same meaning is after *film*, but the cadence of the sentence makes this awkward. Moving *secretly* to anywhere else in the sentence (*The police installed roadside cameras secretly to film motorists speeding* or *The police installed roadside cameras to film motorists speeding secretly*) produces either an ambiguous or unwittingly comic effect. The safest rule seems to be: Avoid splitting an infinitive if you can do so without sounding strange or stilted.

Form Your Verbs: Conjugation

Verbs are conjugated—that is, they appear in different forms—to express different grammatical functions. The verb "to drive" can be conjugated as:

drive	*drives*
drove	*driving*
driven	

This brings us to the distinction between the **regular** and **irregular** verbs.

Regular verbs conjugate simply:

PRESENT TENSE	PAST TENSE	PRESENT PARTICIPLE	PAST PARTICIPLE
I watch	*I watched*	*watching*	*watched*
you watch	*you watched*		
he/she/it watches	*he/she/it watched*		
we watch	*we watched*		
you watch	*you watched*		
they watch	*they watched*		

Irregular verbs, on the other hand, form their past tense and their participle in . . . well, irregular ways.

Sometimes they form the past tense by adding -*t* instead of -*ed* and sometimes by changing the word completely:

dwell/dwelt   *feel/felt*
speak/spoke   *think/thought*

There is no rule for these formations. The example of *speak/spoke* doesn't sanction *squeak/squoke*. There are also verbs with two permissible past-tense formations (which sometimes reflects the difference between British and American English):

burn/burned/burnt   *dream/dreamed/dreamt*
lean/leaned/leant

Irregular verbs—and there are around 200 of them—just have to be learnt . . . sorry, learned.

Now and Then: Tenses

As with most other languages, English indicates time through the use of verbal tenses or the use of helping verbs. Strictly speaking, English has only two pure tenses, the present:

I enjoy.

And the past:

I enjoyed.

The future is constructed by using *will* or, occasionally, *shall,* plus other helping verbs. All the other tenses are also constructed in the same way.

Verbs Have a Voice

Transitive verbs are expressed in two **voices,** the active and the passive.

How Tense Are You?

The following is a list of all English tenses:

Present simple: I enjoy.

Present progressive: I am enjoying.

Present perfect: I have enjoyed.

Present perfect progressive: I have been enjoying.

Simple past: I enjoyed.

Imperfect: I used to enjoy.

Past progressive: I was enjoying.

Past perfect: I had enjoyed.

Future: I shall enjoy.

Future perfect: I shall have enjoyed.

Future progressive: I shall be enjoying.

Future perfect progressive: I shall have been enjoying.

Depending on how it's used, the last can be extremely tortuous, and another tense—the future perfect, for instance—may well be preferable.

Shall We Dance?

Today we rarely use *shall*. In fact, few of us would even know when its use would be appropriate. In general, *will* is the helping verb to express the future tense, but *shall* comes in handy if you're asking a first-person question and soliciting an opinion or approval: "Shall I make dinner now?" "Shall we go to visit your grandmother?" It can be used to make any question sound more formal— "Shall I eat the rest of the pizza?"—Or to add emphasis: "I shall eat all the pizza."

In the active voice the subject of the sentence "does"; in the passive voice the subject "is done to":

Lee Harvey Oswald assassinated President Kennedy. (**active**)

President Kennedy was assassinated by Lee Harvey Oswald. (**passive**)

For more on active and passive voice, see page 136.

. . . And Moods, Too

Mood in the grammatical sense has nothing to do with moodiness. It is a corruption of the word *mode* and is the form of a verb that expresses how the action of the verb is represented. There are five moods: **indicative, imperative, subjunctive, optative,** and **interrogative.**

In the indicative, the verb acts as a statement of fact:

The dollar has fallen against the yen.

In the imperative, as a command:

Get out of here now.

In the subjunctive, as an indica-
tion of unreality (the action of the
verb hasn't happened yet or doesn't
exist. It might simply be a wish, a
suggestion, or a requirement, or it
may be imaginary):

If I were to win the lottery.

In the optative, as a wish:

May you always be happy.

> **Cliché Clock**
>
> A number of set phrases, or clichés, that have survived
> from the past are still couched in the subjunctive mood:
>
> *far be it from me*   *come what may*
> *the powers that be*

And in the interrogative, as a question:

Have you had dinner?

In other languages, each mood has its own verb form. In English the moods are almost always expressed by sentence construction and the use of helping verbs. The exception is the subjunctive, which distinguishes itself with the verb *to be* ("were" instead of "was" in "If I were to win the lottery") and in the third-person singular of other verbs:

The board demanded that he resign immediately.

Adjectives

> *"The man . . . taught me to distrust adjectives as I
> would later learn to distrust certain people."*
> —ERNEST HEMINGWAY, *A MOVEABLE FEAST*,
> WRITING OF EZRA POUND
>
> *"As to the adjective, when in doubt, strike it out."*
> —MARK TWAIN, *PUDD'NHEAD WILSON*

Adjectives get bad press—deservedly. Because their role is to "describe," you may be tempted to think they are all you need to create powerful prose. They are not. The overuse of adjectives clogs up sentences, making them difficult to read and understand. Hemingway's misgiving is a good one to bear in mind.

All the same, you are unlikely to write much more than a short paragraph without needing to use an adjective. The above paragraph contains two: "bad" in the first sentence and "good" in the last (as well as "difficult" in the adjectival clause). They are both examples of how adjectives seduce you into imprecise thinking and writing. "Bad press" is, in any case, a modern cliché. "Hostile press" might be better. "Good one" is wretchedly vague. How about "helpful," "instructive," or "illuminating" instead? Almost anything is better than "good." Fire that author. But sometimes you can get away with it. Here is a sentence that is almost all adjectives:

"When I'm good, I'm very good, but when I'm bad I'm better." —Mae West

Since it's difficult to avoid them, you might as well know what adjectives do. They modify nouns. That is, they add something that the noun alone does not tell you:

a beautiful woman
a fat man
a fierce dog

Not all dogs are fierce, not all men are fat, not all women are beautiful—and not all adjectives modify the noun to which they are attached. The phrase *a mere child* tells you nothing about the child but instead describes the *state* of childhood. In the phrase *a heavy drinker*, it is not the drinker who is heavy, but his drinking.

Adjectives can be used before the noun (the attributive position):

an enormous bill

Or after the noun, plus verb (the predicate position):

The bill was enormous.

They can be used as comparatives and superlatives by adding -er, -est, *more*, or *most*:

bigger/biggest
duller/dullest
more glorious/most glorious

Furthermore, adjectives themselves can be modified by other words:

grossly irresponsible   *rather attractive*
so useful   *very large*

Nouns can sometimes modify other nouns, but they still remain nouns:

Morse code   *evening gown*
machine tool

To figure out if a noun is serving as an adjective, the test is whether you can say, "This code is Morse," "This dress is evening," or "This tool is machine." You can't (except questionably in the first example), so your answer is that they serve only as nouns.

Whole phrases and clauses can act as adjectives:

Wagner's operas are unendurably long.
   (*Unendurably long* is an adjectival phrase.)
Wagner's music is better than it sounds.
   (*better than it sounds* is an adjectival clause.)

The present and past participles of verbs can also act as adjectives:

parting shot (present participle of *to part*)
a vanished civilization (past participle of *to vanish*)

Adverbs

Adverbs do to verbs what adjectives do to nouns—they add something to the verb's meaning. But, clever little things, they can also do it to adjectives and other adverbs. They do this in three ways.

A **manner** adverb describes how the action of the verb is being performed. Most manner adverbs end in "ly," but not all:

She inquired eagerly after his whereabouts.
I drive fast.

A **time** adverb gives a time to the action of the verb:

He left yesterday.
I go often to baseball games.
We'll be leaving soon.

A **place** adverb places the action of the verb:

They live nearby.   *There is trouble ahead.*
It must be somewhere.

Most manner adverbs can be qualified by modifying words
(which are also adverbs—adverbs modify adverbs, and by
the way, adverbs also modify adjectives):

She inquired <u>almost</u> eagerly after his whereabouts.
I drive <u>extremely</u> fast.

Most other adverbs cannot be modified, but there are some
exceptions:

We'll be leaving <u>quite</u> soon.
Do you go to the theater <u>very</u> often?

Whole clauses can act as adverbs:

As soon as I've finished this, I will join you.

"As soon as I've finished this" is an adverbial clause (see
also page 59).

Some adverbs—like *probably, surely,* and *certainly*—modify
whole sentences:

I will probably go home before midnight.
It is certainly wrong to say that.

Like adjectives, adverbs can be overused. They are also fa-
mously susceptible to redundancy, which means saying the
same thing twice:

He yelled loudly.   **He whispered quietly.**

Or they can go to the other extreme and contradict the
word they modify, a device usually employed in irony and
comedy:

"I am a deeply superficial person." —Andy Warhol

Adverbs may appear almost anywhere in a sentence, but the
general rule is that a modifying word should go as close to
the word it modifies as possible: "He gazed bleakly at the

scene" is much clearer and smoother than "Bleakly he gazed at the scene." However, a misplaced adverb can sometimes distort the meaning of a sentence or change it entirely. This is especially true when it comes to *only* and *even*:

He only intended to frighten her, not to kill her.

This is incorrect because *only* is modifying the verb *intended,* but it should be modifying the clause *to frighten her*:

He intended only to frighten her, not to kill her.

Likewise:

He even enjoys American Idol.

This should be:

He enjoys even American Idol.

The misuse of *only* and *even* is now so widespread that the correct use often sounds awkward. If you choose the right noun and the right verb in the first place, you will be less likely to need adverbs or adjectives to reinforce your words and clarify your meaning. As a useful exercise, read through every passage that you write, delete every adjective and adverb, read the passage again, and reinstate the missing words only when the meaning has suffered.

Pronouns

Pronouns stand in for nouns and are used to avoid repeating the noun ad nauseam. Some of them still retain the remnants of gender and case—variant forms expressing the word's function in the sentence. There are eight types of pronouns, some displaying gender and case and some not. It seems simplest just to take the whole bunch in sequence.

You, Me and Us: Personal Pronouns

I, you, he, she, it, we, and *they* are the *nominative* case of the personal pronouns; in other words, the case in which they appear when they are the subject of a verb:

"I think, therefore I am."
> —René Descartes, *Discours de la Méthode*

Closed Case

In many languages, cases are different forms of the same word, usually with a changed ending, that express its relationship to the other words in the sentence. In English, instead of giving words different cases, we express their functions by word order and by the use of prepositions. However, pronouns still display case—the subjective (he), objective (him), and possessive (his).

When they are the object of a verb, they appear in the **accusative case**: *me, you, him, her, it, us,* and *them.* So:

The enemy took us unawares.

You and *it* do not appear in a different accusative form. Nor does *it* have a plural of its own, becoming simply *they* or *them. Thou* used to be the second-person-singular pronoun, but it is now obsolete.

What's That? Interrogative Pronouns

Interrogative pronouns—*who, whom, what,* and *which*—are used to ask questions:

Who told you that?
Whom did you tell?
What are you talking about?
Which party do you support?

That's as May Be: Relative Pronouns

Relative pronouns—*who, whom, whose, which,* and *that*—
"relate" to the words they modify and introduce a relative
clause (see also page 61, "It's All Relative."):

The person who gave me the note was not present.
The jacket that I wore was blue.
The man whose house flooded is staying with relatives.
The glass that fell off the shelf shattered into pieces.

Nothing at All: Indefinite Pronouns

Indefinite pronouns are those that replace nouns without
being specific. These include *all, another, any, anyone, any-*
thing, each, everyone, everything, few, many, no one, nobody,
none, nothing, one, several, some, somebody and *someone*:

There was nobody at home.
I know nothing.

That's So: Demonstrative Pronouns

The words *this, that, these,* and *those* are demonstrative
pronouns, indicating something without naming it:

Don't do that, Robert.
That isn't true.

But the same words can act "demonstratively" in conjunction with a noun:

I love that dog!

Sentence Strategy

There is no gender-inclusive third-person-singular pronoun. In a sentence like "Everyone has his own opinion," you have to opt for *his* or *her.* Some people try to choose the gender-neutral alternative: "Everyone has their own opinion." This is now so widespread as to be unstoppable, but a moment's reflection shows it to be contradictory. *Everyone* is singular, but *their* is plural.

There are some sentence strategies to get around this problem.

1. Change the subject to a plural noun and then use a plural pronoun. "All the speakers had their own opinions" is grammatically fine.

2. Get rid of the pronoun. "Everyone has an opinion in this case."

3. Use *his or her* instead of *their.* "Everyone has his or her opinion." Don't resort to this strategy too often or your writing will get clunky, but it will definitely serve to get you out of a tricky spot from time to time.

Suit Yourself: Reflexive Pronouns

Reflexive pronouns are those that are formed by adding -*self* or -*selves* to the basic pronoun. These include *myself, yourself, himself, herself, itself, ourselves, yourselves,* and *themselves.*

As the object of the verb, their function is to "reflect" the subject:

She saw herself in the mirror.
Behave yourself!
We enjoyed ourselves.

Reflexive pronouns can also be used merely to emphasize the role of the subject:

You must shoulder the responsibility yourself.

Love One Another: Reciprocal Pronouns

The words *each other* and *one another* are examples of reciprocal pronouns. *Each other* is used for a reciprocal relationship between two people or things:

They loved each other.

One another is used for more than two:

They all loved one another.

Mine, All Mine: Possessive Pronouns

Pronouns that indicate ownership or possession are possessive pronouns. *My, your, his, her, its, our,* and *their* precede the noun to which they refer:

This is my coat.   **Let's go to your place.**

The forms *mine, yours, his, hers, ours,* and *theirs* usually come after the noun:

This coat is mine.   **Is this car yours?**

. . . But not always:

Mine is the last example to follow.

Prepositions

"Never use a preposition to end a sentence with."
                                                    —Anonymous

Prepositions are words used in front of nouns and pronouns to indicate where one thing is in relation to another:

He put the book on the table.

On is the preposition here. Others examples include *across, after, along, around, at, behind, by, down, for, from, in, near, off, over, past, through, to, under, up, with, in front of,* and *out of.* (The last two are called "complex prepositions" because they consist of more than one word.)

Prepositions are useful and flexible. Consider the sentence:

The quick brown fox jumped over the lazy dog.

The preposition *over* could simply be replaced by *across, around, at, away from, behind, in front of, off, onto,* or *past*—entirely altering the meaning of the sentence. Although useful, prepositions have also become embroiled in one of English grammar's oldest caveats, as quoted at the head of this section—the rule that you should not use a preposition at the end of a sentence. As per the great lexicographer Henry Fowler:

> **"It was once a cherished superstition that prepositions must be kept true to their name and placed before the word they govern in spite of the incurable English instinct for putting them late."**

But even now you cannot entirely disregard the superstition and obey your incurable instincts. "What are you talking about?" is certainly preferable to "About what are you talking?" On the other hand, "This position is one from which we cannot retreat" is preferable to "This position is one that we cannot retreat from."

As with the split infinitive, my advice would be to avoid the terminal preposition unless the alternative sounds cumbersome or ridiculous.

Conjunctions

Conjunctions, as their name suggests, are words that join. They can be used to link phrases, clauses, and sentences, and they do so in four ways.

Coordinating conjunctions join two roughly equal parts of a sentence:

I'm a Mets fan, <u>but</u> you're a Yankees fan.
I have ten fingers <u>and</u> two ears.

The coordinating conjunctions are: *and, but, for, nor, or, so,* and *yet.*

Subordinating conjunctions link a main clause and a subordinate clause (see pages 59–62):

I can't pay you today, <u>because</u> it will drain my bank account.
I'll try to pay you this week, <u>although</u> it will drain my bank account.

Correlative conjunctions work in pairs:

I admire <u>not only</u> her looks but also her wit and intelligence.
You can be <u>either</u> a believer or an unbeliever.
I like <u>both</u> wines <u>and</u> spirits.

As you would expect in words that join the parts of a sentence, their position is crucial to clear expression. In the sentence "I own not only a Ferrari but also a Porsche," the first correlative conjunction—*not only*—comes after the verb, because both types of car are the object of the verb *own*. In the sentence "I not only own a Ferrari but also drive it with exceptional skill," *not only* must come before the verb if the meaning is to be clear, because when taking the sentence as a whole, *I* is the subject of two different verbs—*own* and *drive*—and the two clauses have separate meanings.

Compound conjunctions consist of more than one word but perform a single function:

I will come down <u>as soon</u> as I am ready.
Take <u>as long</u> as you want.
Please arrange the seating <u>so that</u> I don't have sit near my mother-in-law.

Sentence Strategy
While and *Although*

The conjunction *while* normally indicates time, as in "I can wait while you get ready." Sometimes, however, it's given the same meaning as "although," as in "While I like him, I can't stand his politics." There is nothing incorrect in this usage, but it can give rise to some confusion:

While I watch television, my wife reads books.

Here, *while* could mean either *although* or *at the same time as.* It seems simpler to reserve *while* for its time sense if there's any chance of confusion.

Interjections!

Wow! Interjections are words that occur by themselves, often outside a sentence, and take their meaning from tone and content rather than from formal definition. Almost all curse words are interjections, as are *aaargh, boo, yikes, ouch, whoops, whoa*—you get the picture. Hooray!

Articles and Particles

These small but perfectly formed words are nonetheless indispensable.

Articles indicate whether the following noun or phrase is definite or indefinite. English has two articles. The definite article, *the,* can be either singular or plural:

The sun is shining.
The stars in the Milky Way number billions.

The indefinite article, *a* or *an,* is singular:

an awkward moment

A is normally used to precede words beginning with a consonant and *an* to precede words beginning with a vowel. The main exceptions are the silent *h*:

"For Brutus is an honourable man."
                    —William Shakespeare, *Julius Caesar*

. . . and the long *u* sound when it implies the use of the consonant *y*:

a European
a unique opportunity

Because *a* and *an* have no plural form, the indefinite article is merely dropped before a plural:

A European but *Europeans*
A unique opportunity but *unique opportunities*

Particles are generally short words, usually prepositions or adverbs, attached to verbs that change the meaning of the verb. Usually, verbs take only one particle, but there are some two-particle verbs:

She gave <u>in</u> to his demands for more soup and nuts.
I'm going to run <u>out of</u> soup and nuts.
He has fouled <u>up</u> this time.

Grammar

The purpose of speech and writing is to convey meaning. Grammar is how you assemble the parts of speech to do this. The concerns of grammar are inflection, phonetics, and syntax—technical terms for very simple propositions.

Inflection means merely the different forms that words assume. For instance, the noun *house* has two inflected forms: *house* and *houses*. Cases of pronouns and tenses and participles of verbs are all examples of inflection. English is mercifully a little-inflected language. Try Turkish, which has so many inflections that it is possible to express whole sentences in one word—if you wish to.

Phonetics deals with pronunciation and the sound of words (see pages 77–80).

See What's Trending?

Grammar is a moving target. Not only do small things continuously evolve—like words coming in and out of fashion and meanings drifting with usage—but changes in the rules of speech occur as well. In the long run, usage decides the legitimacy of a meaning or a construction.

Syntax deals with the arrangement of words in sentences, or sentence construction.

Inflection and phonetics are sometimes combined in **morphology,** or the structure of words, so grammar can neatly be seen as the science of word and sentence structure.

Phrases

Sentences are larger grammatical units built up from smaller combinations of words—phrases and clauses.

Phrases are the simplest combinations of words. A phrase is any combination of words that can't stand alone as a sentence (because it lacks a subject and a predicate, see page 63) but nonetheless forms a single grammatical unit. There are five types of phrases, related to the parts of speech they employ.

A **noun phrase** assumes the role of a noun, as subject, direct object, or the object of a preposition:

Almost all men dislike doing the dishes. (*Almost all men* is a noun phrase and the subject of *dislike*.)

It isn't true that most women dislike <u>almost all men.</u> (*almost all men* is the object.)

Goodwill to <u>almost all men</u>. (*almost all men* is the object of the preposition *to*.)

A **verb phrase** is any group of words that follow a subject. Think of a noun—*elephant*—and add a phrase after it; that's your verb phrase.

The elephant <u>has a phenomenal memory</u>.

The elephant <u>will eat as much hay as it can reach with its trunk</u>.

In the first example, *has a phenomenal memory* is the verb phrase. In the second, the entire *will eat as much hay as it can reach with its trunk* is the verb phrase.

Verb phrases can also be formed around participles and infinitives, sometimes called **participle phrases** and **infinitive phrases**:

Having to fill out tax forms **is** *to enter the third circle of hell*. (*Having to fill out tax forms* **is a participle phrase, while** *to enter the third circle of hell* **is an infinitive phrase**).

An **adjective phrase** behaves like an adjective and qualifies, or modifies, nouns:

She was *as clever as* *her father but* *prettier than* *her mother.*

An **adverb phrase** does the same but acts as an adverb:

I reached the top *more quickly than most.*

And a **prepositional phrase** uses a preposition plus a noun or a noun phrase:

Many rare plants are to be found *in the botanical gardens.*

"The General was essentially a man of peace, <u>except in his domestic life.</u>"
    —Oscar Wilde, *The Importance of Being Earnest*

Clauses

Clauses are to phrases as bacteria are to viruses. They are more complex and capable of independent existence. Like a sentence, a clause must contain a subject and predicate with a finite verb. There are six types of clauses.

A **main clause** can stand alone as a simple sentence:

I feel lousy.

It can also become a clause in a more complex sentence containing other clauses. It is common for an English sentence to have two or more main clauses, and these are called **coordinating clauses**:

<u>*I feel lousy*</u> *because* <u>*I have the flu*</u>.

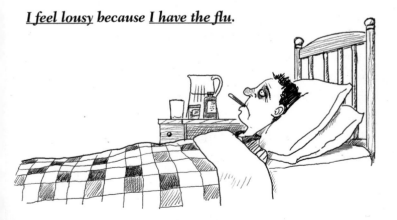

This sentence has two main coordinating clauses (each can stand alone as a sentence)—*I feel lousy* and *I have the flu*—linked by the conjunction *because*.

When part of a sentence cannot stand alone, it is called a **dependent clause**:

I feel lousy in spite of <u>the medicine I took</u>.

Here *the medicine I took* is a subordinate clause, because it cannot stand alone despite having a noun and a verb. *In spite of* is a prepositional phrase modifying *the medicine I took*.

Dangling clauses

When you combine clauses, there's always the risk that you'll leave one dangling unhappily, not related to the rest of the sentence. In dependent clauses the name gives a hint: The dependent clause "depends" on the main clause and has to agree with it.

Running furiously, the train pulled out of the
*   station before Stacy could leap aboard.*

There's more wrong here than the fact that Stacy, in her rush to make the train, left her suitcase behind in the taxi. The dependent clause—*running furiously*—is meant to describe something or, in this case, someone: Stacy. But here *running furiously* is a dangling participle (a form of a verb functioning as an adjective) describing the subject of the sentence, *the train*. Oops.

You can rephrase this sentence any number of ways to avoid the curse of the dangling participle. Here are two solutions:

Running furiously, Stacy missed the train as it pulled out of the station.

The train pulled out of the station before Stacy, running furiously, could leap aboard.

It's All Relative

Clauses introduced by one of the relative pronouns—*who, whom, whose, which,* and *that*—are called **relative clauses**:

I know the man <u>who broke the bank at Monte Carlo</u>.

<u>Whichever way you look at it</u>, the situation is a disaster.

Sentence Strategy

"When choosing between two evils, I always like to take the one I've never tried before." —MAE WEST

Neat sentences keep their dependents close to the object they're dependent on. In the sentence above, *When choosing between two evils* describes Mae West, who had a penchant for crossing the line, and that clause is right next to *I,* the subject of the sentence. When in doubt, put your clause near your subject and make sure it makes sense.

Relative clauses can be divided into **restrictive** and **nonrestrictive** clauses. Restrictive clauses define something in the main clause and are necessary in order to gain a full understanding of the sentence. Nonrestrictive clauses are not essential but merely add extra information.

The flowers <u>that you sent</u> were very gratefully received. (**restrictive**)

The law, <u>which had been in discussion for six months,</u> was passed by a large majority. (**nonrestrictive**)

Sentences

The sentence is the largest grammatical unit in English and should contain (there are, of course, exceptions) a subject, verb, and object. Verb, object, and everything else except the subject are called, collectively, the **predicate.** Normally a sentence starts with a capital letter and ends with a period, a question mark, or an exclamation point.

Sentences consist of **phrases** and **clauses.** A **simple sentence** consists of a single clause:

He stole my car.

He is the subject, *stole* is the verb, *my car* is the object, and *stole my car* is the predicate.

A **compound sentence** consists of two main clauses:

He stole my car, and the police pursued him.

That Which We Should Know

If the relative clause is an aside—in other words, a nonrestrictive clause—use *which* and always surround the clause with commas:

The facts, which he had known for a long time, were conclusive.

If the relative clause is an essential part of the sentence—a restrictive clause—use *that* without commas:

The information that you gave me was unreliable.

A **complex sentence** consists of a main clause and a subordinate clause:

> *"But here, unless I am mistaken, is our client."*
> —Arthur Conan Doyle, *Wisteria Lodge*

Unless I am mistaken is the subordinate clause, because it can be removed without affecting the meaning of the sentence.

A **compound complex sentence** scatters clauses and phrases about like confetti. The longest published sentence in English is Molly Bloom's soliloquy in *Ulysses* by James Joyce, which runs to 4,391 words. Here is a more manageable compound complex sentence:

> *"It is my belief, Watson, founded upon my experience, that the lowest and vilest alleys of London do not present a more dreadful record of sin than does the smiling and beautiful countryside."*
> —Arthur Conan Doyle, *The Copper Beeches*

It is my belief is the first main clause; *Watson* is an interjection; *founded upon my experience* is a subordinate clause; *that* is a conjunction; from *the lowest* to *sin* is the second main clause; *than* is a conjunction; and from *does* to *countryside* is the third main clause. All three main clauses are coordinating clauses. That's 33 words. Imagine more than 4,000.

There are four types of sentences:

A **declarative sentence** makes a simple statement:
I went to the supermarket.

An **interrogative sentence** asks a question:
Did you go to the supermarket?

An **imperative sentence** issues a command:
Go nowhere near the supermarket.

An **exclamatory sentence** makes an exclamation:
Just look at the supermarket!

All sentences must have a subject. However, an imperative sentence is the exception to the rule; the second person is implied in the command:

[You] go nowhere near the supermarket.

Not all imperatives are threatening:

Make someone's day with a bunch of flowers.

Fragments are groups of words without a verb that are nonetheless used like sentences, usually in speech and often in reply to a question:

"Where did you put my book?"
"Back on the shelf."

Subjects and Objects

In a standard, straightforward sentence, the normal sequence is subject, verb, object:

I love you.

But this rule is not written in stone. Sometimes the object may come first or the verb may precede the subject, especially in questions and informal speech.

This I can do without.
Which coat can you do without?

Returning the Complement

In saying "It is my belief," Sherlock Holmes uses the verb *to be.* It is tempting to see *my belief* as the object, but it's not. The verb *to be* is the most important of the **copulative verbs.** In addition to giving grammarians an excuse to  snicker, copulative verbs express a state rather than perform an action. For this reason, the subject of this sentence cannot take an object and instead has to make due with a complement. So *my belief* is the complement of *It is,* because *It* and *my belief* are the same thing. Copulative verbs indicate that the two parts of the sentence are the same thing or share a quality. Some of the most common copulative verbs are *become, seem,* and *taste.*

> *He has become very deaf.*
> *It seems strange.*
> *That tastes disgusting.*

It is also possible for the subject of a copulative verb to be singular while the complement is plural, and vice versa. The verb agrees in number with the subject, not the complement.

> *Books are my chief interest.*
> *My chief interest is books.*

Sentence Strategy

When personal pronouns are used as the complement of the verb to be, they are always in the nominative case.

It was she. (except her)

It was I. (and me)

Sometimes this rule is blurred in casual use. Leaving a phone message, you might easily say, "Hi, it's me." Saying "It's I" sounds strange and formal.

A sentence can also have more than one object. This can be in the form of two direct objects:

He lost his hat and gloves.

He lost his hat and his temper. (This—usually jocular—construction, using two objects that reflect slightly different applications of the verb, is known as zeugma or syllepsis.)

Or a direct object and an indirect object:

He paid me the compliment of taking me seriously.

Here *the compliment* is the direct object and *me* is the indirect object. This seems the wrong way around, but in fact the sentence is saying "paid a compliment to me."

Sentences can also have more than one subject. They both act as subjects, and the personal pronoun, if present, should be in the nominative case:

My husband and I wish you all a merry Christmas.

Not *My husband and me,* and certainly not *Me and my husband.*

Agreement

English verbs must agree with their subject in number. When two or more subjects are connected by *and,* the verb goes in the plural:

My wife and my son <u>are</u> going away for Christmas.

If the subjects are connected by a conjunction that implies they are not doing the same thing, the verb goes in the singular:

I don't know if my wife or my son <u>is</u> going away for Christmas.

The constructions *either/or* and *neither/nor* always precede a singular verb:

Neither my wife nor my son <u>is</u> going away for Christmas.

An intervening subordinate clause does not affect the verb:

My wife, as well as both my sons, <u>is</u> going away for Christmas.

My *wife* remains the subject, and the verb remains singular.

Some words that look like modifiers are actually pronouns and also function as the subject of the verb, with which they must agree in number:

Each of these dogs <u>is</u> well trained. (not *are*, as the plural *dogs* might lead you to expect; the subject is *Each*.)

Every dog <u>has</u> its day.

Each and *every*, along with *anybody, anyone, everybody, everyone, one, somebody,* and *someone,* are always singular. A *few, both,* and *several* are always plural. But *all, any, most,* and *some* may be either singular or plural. As with *less* and *fewer,* it depends on the noun, so countable nouns take the plural, uncountable nouns the singular:

Any guilty persons <u>are</u> to be arrested.
Any residue <u>is</u> to be removed.
All cats <u>are</u> gray in the dark.
All darkness <u>is</u> welcome to cats.
Most of the money <u>is</u> still missing.
Most of the coins <u>are</u> counterfeit.

The word *many* is almost always plural.

Numerical expressions, like collective nouns, may be singular or plural, depending on whether a single unit or a collection of individuals is referenced:

The number of people present <u>was</u> vast.
A vast number of people <u>were</u> present.
Ten dollars <u>is</u> too much for a haircut.
Ten dollars <u>are</u> burning a hole in my pocket.
Five years <u>is</u> a long time.
The five years since then <u>have been</u> the longest of
    my life.

The subject always governs the number of the verb, but you can find many sentences (and write many sentences) that use constructions in which the subject gets "lost" and the verb is given an incorrect number. This happens frequently with constructions using "number" words, like *average, maximum, minimum,* and *total,* which can take either a singular or a plural. Again, the difference is between a single unit and a number:

A *maximum of ten people is* allowed to use this elevator. (*are* is tempting, but *maximum* is the subject, and singular.)

The minimum number of points necessary to pass the test is fifty.

An *average of 20,000 people logs on to my website each day* (the ear rebels at *people* followed by a singular verb even though it is correct. The difficulty can be avoided by saying "About 20,000 people log on to my website each day").

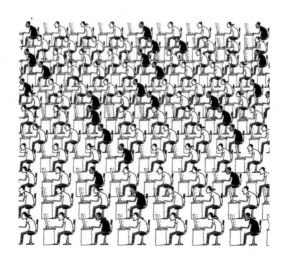

Where a conjunction like *of* is absent and a number is being referred to, the verb should take the plural:

Maximum temperatures <u>were</u> well over ninety degrees.

Agreement in Case

Verbs, their subjects, and their objects must agree not only in number but also in case. This rule applies mainly to pronouns, and confusion most often occurs when there is a "missing" verb or other missing words:

You're a better man than <u>I</u>.

The personal pronoun goes in the nominative or subjective case—*I*—because the verb *am* (as in "You're a better man than I am, Gunga Din!"—Rudyard Kipling) is understood, or hidden.

But a hidden verb can also take an object:

I like him almost as much as <u>her</u>.

Read "almost as much as <u>I like</u> her," the *I like* is hidden and *her* is its object.

When the personal pronoun follows the word *but*, it should be in the case it would have been in if the "hidden" verb were supplied:

I managed to flunk my driving test six times. Who but <u>I</u>?

Here "Who but <u>I would do that</u>" is implied.

They have no allies but <u>us</u>.

Here the verb is supplied. As *us* is the indirect object of *have*, it therefore takes the accusative or objective case.

The same rule of agreement applies to comparatives and superlatives:

Which of you two is the <u>elder</u>? (**not** *eldest*)

It was impossible to decide which of the three was the <u>eldest</u>.

The issue of agreement raises the question of simplicity. If you find yourself mired in relative clauses, hidden verbs, complex tenses, and problems of case, go back to the simple rule—subject, verb, object—and rewrite your thoughts more simply. It is sometimes possible to lose track of your meaning entirely.

Sentence Strategy

The relative pronouns *who* and *whom* must also agree in case. When used in a relative clause that modifies the subject of the main clause, it should be in the subjective case:

He who hesitates is lost.

Here, *he* and *who* must agree, because *who hesitates* is a relative clause modifying *he,* the subject.

But here's another example:

I was avoiding the man whom my dog had bitten.

Whom my dog had bitten is a relative clause modifying the object (*the man*) of the verb (*was avoiding*), so it takes the objective case.

It's easy to be confused as to whether to use *who* or *whom* in a sentence. For example, there is a temptation to use *whom* in the following:

I was never in any doubt about who was the culprit.

Resist the temptation, however, because *who* is the subject of *was,* not the object of *about.*

Phonetics and Spelling

> "If there is one thing certain about English pronunciation,
> it is that there is almost nothing certain about it."
> —BILL BRYSON, *MOTHER TONGUE*

If you have struggled with Latin declensions, French genders, or German irregular verbs, now is the moment to take revenge. The spelling and pronunciation of English words are without any vestige of method or even common sense. English contains more words spelled the same way but pronounced differently than any other language.

Take, for instance, the notorious example of the letters *ough*. They can be pronounced in no fewer than nine entirely separate ways: lough (*och*, as in "och aye"), bough (*ow*), thorough (*uh*), though (*o*), thought (*or*), tough (*uff*), through (*oo*), and trough (*off*).

Same Spelling, Different Pronunciation—or Vice Versa?

Contemplate the following words, all containing the same elements of spelling and all pronounced differently:

ache/apache *know/how*
break/streak *leak/steak*
five/give *maid/said*
heard/beard *moll/roll*
height/weight *road/broad*
hour/pour *sieve/grieve*

Then there are words spelled differently but pronounced the same, or at least with the same vowel sound—a very long list, of which this is just a mere sampling:

brake/break
choke/folk
leak/leek
plain/plane

The erratic nature of English spelling should be no surprise. English is a river fed by many streams. The parent language, Anglo-Saxon, even as it arrived in England, absorbed some—admittedly very few—Celtic words, mainly place names. Then, as the Danes and other Norsemen raided and subsequently settled up to a third of Britain, the language absorbed a huge number of Scandinavian words.

Modern English was made in the centuries following the Norman Conquest, as Norman French was absorbed into the existing Anglo-Saxon/Scandinavian mix, transforming the language into the potent, word-rich brew that we now use.

To these must be added the classical languages—Greek and Latin—whose influence on English has been immense: indirectly via the classical roots of Norman French, and directly via the medieval Church and through the emphasis on Greek and Latin in the educational system of the eighteenth and nineteenth centuries.

So we inherit words from at least four major roots, plus innumerable minor infusions from all over the world as the British embarked on their maritime and, later, territorial empire—Spanish, French, Italian, Portuguese, Hindi, Persian, Arabic, Dutch, Chinese, Gaelic, Afrikaans, Swahili, Native American languages, Australian aboriginal languages, Zulu, and many others.

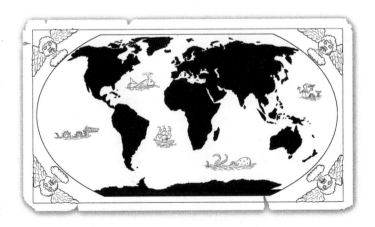

As all these influences flooded into English, there was never any system to reconcile their pronunciation with an agreed spelling. Also, unusually for a parent language, English has been content largely to leave the spelling of imported words in its native form. In the meantime, the dispersal of English speakers over the globe, often to distant and isolated communities, further fragmented and diversified English pronunciation.

Given this confused picture, it seems sensible simply to list the main points that give rise to confusion about spelling and pronunciation in English. At each point some general tendency will emerge, but these are never hard-and-fast rules, and many exceptions will be found.

Before and After: Prefixes and Suffixes

A prefix is a group of letters that can be added to the beginning of a word to change its meaning. There are many possible prefixes, among them *pre-* itself. Other common examples include *anti-*, *circum-*, *demi-*, *dis-*, *extra-*, *inter-*, *re-*, *sub-*, *trans-*, and *un-*.

Usually the prefix is tacked on to the beginning of the parent word without altering the spelling:

dissatisfied   *overregulated*

Your New Best Friend

Meet the dictionary! Perhaps you were acquainted long, long ago and fell out of touch? Dictionaries are invaluable tools for good writers. They allow you to check spellings, word breaks, and meanings.

But not always:

dispirited   *transubstantiation*

And when the words *all* and *well* are the prefixes, the second *l* is always dropped:

altogether   *welfare*

The prefixes *dis-*, *il-*, *im-*, *in-*, *ir-*, *mis-*, and *un-* reverse the meaning of the parent word:

disillusioned   *illogical*
impossible   *indefatigable*
irresponsible   *misappropriate*
unnatural

But different prefixes often result in differing meanings:

disaffected/unaffected   *disuse/misuse*
disinterested/uninterested

Sometimes an "opposite" formed by attaching a prefix to a stem word becomes a widespread, much-used word, while the stem word falls into disuse until revived by a master hand:

"If not actually disgruntled, he was far from being gruntled." —Humorist P. G. Wodehouse

A suffix is a group of letters added to the end of a word. Suffixes include *-able, -ant, -ation, -ent, -ful,- fy,- ible, -ing,- ize, -ist, -ity, -ly, -ment,* and *-ness.* Unfortunately, these cause more confusion about spelling than prefixes. If the parent word ends in *y,* the *y* is converted to *i* unless it is preceded by a vowel:

happy/happiness

But:

enjoy/enjoyment

If the word ends in *e,* the *e* is dropped unless doing so would result in a different pronunciation of the word:

mistake/unmistakable

but:

manage/manageable

In some cases both spellings are acceptable, as in *age/ageing/aging*.

The suffixes *-able* and *-ible* mean the same and are used randomly:

illegible   *lovable*
incorrigible   *respectable*

Like irregular verbs, you simply have to learn them or look them up. Their correct use is a dividing line between those taught under the old system of learning by rote and those taught under the "look and guess" system.

The Suffixes *-able* and *-ible*

The suffix *-able* comes from Latin via French, while *-ible* comes directly from Latin. There is no hard-and-fast rule to distinguish whether *-able* or *-ible* is the correct suffix to use to form an adjective. Of the following, two are incorrect. Can you figure out which ones?

combustable   *convertible*
correctible   *designable*
speakable   *usable*

The incorrect spellings were *correctable* and *combustible*. A dictionary is the best source for finding out which spellings are correct.

There are some rules, however, when it comes to adjectives that are formed by adding *-able* to another word:

- If the stem word ends in a silent *e*, it is dropped: *lovable, adorable.* However, if the stem ends in *ce, ee, ge,* or *le*, the final *e* is retained: *agreeable, manageable.* The *e* might be retained if the pronunciation would be altered by dropping it.

- A stem word with a final *y* transposes it to *i*—*reliable* —with the exception of *flyable*, or when the *y* is preceded by a vowel: *enjoy/enjoyable.*

- A stem ending in a consonant usually doubles it— *embeddable*—but there are exceptions: *preferable, transferable* (see below).

- Words of more than two syllables ending in *-ate* usually drop the *-ate*: *calculable, demonstrable.*

- Words ending in *-ible* form their negatives with the prefixes *il-* or *in-*: *illegible, inaccessible.*

The Endings *-ant* and *-ent*

Some words take *-ant* for the noun and *-ent* for the adjectival form: *dependant* is the noun, *dependent* the adjective. Likewise: *descendant/descendent, pendant/pendent. Independent* is both noun and adjective.

The Letters ae and oe

Originally printed as æ and œ, these are now sometimes rendered as two letters. Derived from Latin and Greek, they appear in words like *aesthetic, amoeba,* and *Caesar.*

The Endings *-ative* and *-ive*

Some words form adjectives by adding either *-ative* or *-ive,* but there is no rule. *Authoritative* but a*ssertive, exploitative* but *supportive, quantitative* but *preventive.*

-ede and Supersede

The ending *-cede* is usual in verbs like *concede, intercede, precede* and *recede.* Exceptions are *exceed, proceed* and *succeed.* The suffixes are from the same Latin root—*cedere*—meaning to yield, give way, or go away. Confusingly, and hence often misspelled, there is *supersede* with an *s,* which has a different Latin root—*sedere*—meaning to sit.

Double Your Consonants

When you add a suffix to words ending in a consonant, you double the consonant—or not. It depends on both the word and the suffix. It also depends on where the stress falls in the stem word. The simplest way to explain this "rule" is by example:

- **Bed** *becomes* **bedding** *because there is only one vowel before the final consonant.*

- **Head** *becomes* **heading** *because there are two vowels.*

But it's not the same with words of two or more syllables:

- **Crochet** *becomes* **crocheting** (crowshaying) *because the final t in* **crochet** *is silent.*
- **Occur** *becomes* **occurred** *because the stress falls on the last syllable.*

- **Benefit** *becomes* **benefited** *because the stress falls on the first syllable.*

- **Bias** *becomes* **biased** *because the stress falls on the first syllable.*

Of course, a rule with so many variations and exceptions can barely be called a rule. If in doubt, go to a dictionary.

Indecent and Undressed

The negative particles *in-* and *un-* are used more or less indiscriminately, outside a general tendency for *un-* to go with English root words and *in-* with Latin: *unlovable, unreadable,* but *inadmissible, incontrovertible.* The prefix *in-* takes the forms *il-, im-,* and *ir-* before words beginning with *l*, *m*, and *r*: *illegal, immoderate, irreconcilable.*

It is convenient to have both *in-* and *un-*. In many instances they are combined with the same word to give a subtly different meaning: *inapt/unapt, inhuman/unhuman, immaterial/unmaterial, immoral/unmoral.* There is a tendency for *in-* to favor certain word endings and *un-* others, but there are too many exceptions to make a helpful rule.

-yze, -ise, or -ize?

To make things just a bit more complicated, there are three verb endings that are spelled differently but all pronounced "eyes." They are *-yze, -ise,* and *-ize,* and the difference in spelling is because they come from different root words. The *-yze* endings, like *paralyze* and *analyze,* are derived from Greek and have nouns ending in *-ysis.*

I before e . . .

"*I* before *e* unless after *c*, when it sounds like double *ee*" used to be the spelling mantra in school. And it still holds true: *deceive, receive, field, yield.* Exceptions include *caffeine, codeine, heinous, protein,* and *seize.* Some proper names with the *ee* sound use *ei*: *Keith, Leith, Sheila.* The letters *ie* and *ei* also stand for other sounds: *forfeit, friendly, surfeit, view.*

The verbs of the second group are less easy to spot—those that end in *-ise*. They stem from various different roots, and they include *exercise, improvise, incise, surmise, televise.*

The majority of the "eyes" verbs fall in the third. For these the stem word should end in *-ism*, *-ization*, *-y*, or be a complete word: *criticize, realize, philosophize, computerize.*

To "er" Is Human

As with *-in* and *-un*, the distinction between the endings *-er* and *-or* is between English and Latin. But the choice of ending is also influenced by the form of the stem word, and there is no general rule. The endings are added to verbs to make a noun mean one who does what the verb implies: *controller, debater, walker, councilor, counselor, conqueror.*

The suffix *-or* tends to appear in technical terms—*duplicator, resistor*—and as a legal variant of the *-er* ending—*abettor, mortgagor, vendor.* In addition, *-or* tends to follow the letters *at* in words such as *agitator,* as well as the letter *t—actor, executor, prospector*—while -*er* tends to follow doubled consonants (except *ss*) and other letter combinations. But there are many exceptions. The double *s* is a law unto itself: *fusser, kisser, presser, compressor, professor.*

American English substitutes -*or* for the *our* ending, which is common in British English—*color, humor,* and *labor* rather than *colour, humour,* and *labour.*

Sentence Strategy

Many people try to enliven their writing by turning to an online thesaurus to suggest polysyllabic synonyms, but be warned: The precise meaning of the suggested word may differ slightly, significantly altering the gist of your writing and having beastly consequences. Always do some further research into the suggested word so you can be sure you're saying what you mean.

Say It Straight

> *"The 't' is silent, as in Harlow."*
>
> —PUTDOWN FROM MARGOT ASQUITH TO FILM STAR
> JEAN HARLOW, WHO HAD RASHLY MISPRONOUNCED
> ASQUITH'S FIRST NAME AS "MARGOTT"

Silent letters are indeed a problem, but let's start at the beginning.

The Vowels

A vowel is a sound made by the unimpeded passage of the breath through the mouth. In English you cannot make a syllable without a vowel. The English alphabet contains five vowels—*a, e, i, o,* and *u.* The consonant *y* also appears as a vowel in words like *cry.* But this is by no means the extent of the vowel sounds. English speakers use about 20 vowel sounds, because each of the vowel letters can yield different sounds—by itself, repeated, or joined to other vowels or consonants.

Even by themselves, the vowels yield 11 sounds:

a—as in *apple, father, made*
e—as in *eke* and *else*
i—as in *hit* and *like*
o—as in *doll* and *oh*
u—as in *duke* and *up*

The sound of a vowel is not, in English, tied to the vowel letter. There may be many other ways to represent it. There are, for instance, more than a dozen ways of spelling the long *o* sound: *beau, go, slow, though, toe,* and so on. Similarly, there are many ways to represent the long *a* sound: *bake, great, hay, hey, staid, weight,* and more.

Long or Short *a*

The letter *a* followed by a consonant and a terminal *e* is usually pronounced *ay*: *grade, grate, made, trade.* But in some words of French origin, it is given the French sound, roughly corresponding to *ah*: *dressage, façade, fuselage, garage, promenade.*

In words ending *-ada,* the penultimate *a* is usually short: *armada.* The same applies to words ending in *-ado*: *avocado, bravado, Mikado,* and in *tomato.* Exceptions are *tornado* and *potato,* where it is long.

With other consonants *a* can take on other sounds:

alter, halt, salt: short *o*, as in *doll*
Alsatian, altitude, alto: short *a*, as in *cat*
data, hiatus, ultimatum: long *a*, as in *mate*
errata, sonata: soft *a*, as in *art*

Endings in *-ed*

The suffix *-ed* is sometimes pronounced as a separate syllable—*naked, wicked, wretched*—and sometimes elided (not pronounced), such as in *loved, talked, walked*. The ending can be both pronounced and elided in the same word, giving different meanings—*aged* (very old) or *aged* ("having age" as in "aged 21"), *learned* (knowledgeable) or *learned* (the past of *to learn*).

When *-ed* is paired with other parts of speech—using the *-ly* and *-ness* suffixes—the *ed* takes on a separate syllable:

nakedly/nakedness   *wickedly/wickedness*
wretchedly/wretchedness

And elided if it is suppressed in the stem word:

hurriedly/hurriedness

If the syllable before the *-ed* in the stem word is stressed, the *ed* is pronounced in the adverb:

allegedly   *assuredly*
deservedly

"O" Dear

The short *u* sound, as in *mud,* is often spelled with an *o* in English—*above, come, front, son*—and *o* sometimes appears where the sound may be either *u* or *o,* as in *accomplice* and *mongrel.* Usually *o* followed by a consonant is a short *o* sound, as in *combat, hovel,* and *sojourn.* However, before a double *l,* the *o* is often long: *roll, stroll, swollen.* But not always—*collar, dollar, doll, moll.* Before the letters *lt,* the *o* again becomes long—*bolt, colt, revolt*—but becomes short again in front of *lv*—*involve, revolve, solve.* If you think this is complicated, wait till you get to *u.*

Yoo-hoo

The long *u* sound can usefully be seen as a combination of vowels—the sound *you,* as in *cube, volume,* and *value;* and *oo,* as in *rude.* In the first case—*cube*—there is unmistakably a *y* sound at the front of the vowel. *You* itself is pronounced in the same way as *yew* and *ewe*. The *y* sound is difficult to enunciate after certain consonants and has gradually faded from many English words that previously had it. The *oo* sound is clearly heard in words like *blue, brute, chew, chute, clue, deluge, lewd,* and *substitute.*

The short *u* also has two pronunciations. One as in *hull—bulge, bulk, pulp—*and the other as in *bull—full, fulsome, pull.*

Consonants

A consonant is defined as any letter that is not a vowel.

Consonants are thought of as making "harder" sounds than the vowels, using tongue, lips, and palate in a way that vowels do not. However, of the 21 consonants in the English alphabet, eight sound "soft," or can be pronounced in a "soft" way: *c, f, g, h, r, s, w,* and *y.*

As with vowels, the sounds made by consonants are not always represented by the same letter. The sound represented by *sh,* for instance, can be rendered in a number of ways: *champagne, fission, Mauritius, ocean, shoot, sugar.*

C the Rules

C can be pronounced with a hard sound, like *k—antic, bloc, cake, comedy, cut, incredible, music, uncle—*or a soft sound, like *s—censure, cyanide, ulcer.* A rule of thumb for *c* is that it is usually soft when followed by the vowels *e, i,* and *y* and hardened by *a, o,* and *u.* Thus, we have *electric* and *electricity.* There are, of course, exceptions: *arc* retains its hardness in *arcing.*

Grrr . . . Soft G or Hard?

The initial hard *g* is heard in *gabble, grant, grunt,* and many others. The soft *g* appears in *gem, gibber, gibe.* As with *c,* the rule of thumb is that the letter is softened when followed by the vowels *e* and *i* and hardened when followed by *a, o,* and *u.* If a *g* needs to be hardened, a silent *u* is inserted—as in *analogue, guest, guide, rogue.*

As with all rules, there are exceptions. The correct pronunciation of *margarine* gives it a hard *g,* but it is rarely heard nowadays; the soft *g* sound is preferred. In *gill* and *gig,* for instance, the hard *g* has been retained.

Gynecology and other *gyn* words are pronounced with a hard initial *g*—presumably because its derivation (the Greek *gun,* "woman, female") has a hard *g*—but when the *gyn* occurs inside words, the rule reasserts itself and is spoken with a soft *g*—*misogynist.*

In the *ng* construction the *g* is sometimes sounded, as in *anger* (hard) and *binge* (soft), and sometimes suppressed, as in *banged, longed, or singer.*

Silent Consonants

English abounds in consonants that are not pronounced. In many cases this has to do with the word origins— whether Anglo-Saxon, Old Norse, Old French . . . Adopted into various dialects throughout Britain, these words had no set pronunciations when their spelling was established. Among them are *aisle, eight, folk, gnash, knee, know, would,* and, of course, the *-ough* endings detailed at the start of this chapter.

Other words gained a silent consonant, imposed on an

existing pronunciation in an attempt around the sixteenth century to regularize English spelling and make it conform to the words' Latin origins—*debt, receipt, island, rhyme.*

Renaissance grammarians are responsible for other silent consonants, again introduced to conform to their Latin and/or Greek derivations. The letter *g* is again silent in the *gm* construction, as in *paradigm* and *phlegm.* Likewise, the letter *h* is sometimes silent both as an initial—*heir, honest, hour*—and inside a word—*dishonest, dishonorable, where, which.* In Greek-derived words beginning with *pn-, ps-,* and *pt-,* it is customary not to sound the *p*—*pneumonia, psychology, pterodactyl.*

Compound Consonants

Additional sounds can be made by combining two or sometimes more consonants. This is standard and widespread, and sometimes sounds are duplicated: *sh,* as in shoot, and the soft *ch,* as in champagne; *nks,* as in thanks, and *nx* as in Manx. The main consonant groupings that make sounds not found in the single consonants are (underlined): <u>ch</u>ur<u>ch</u>, bran<u>ch</u>, belo<u>ng</u>, lu<u>ng</u>e, le<u>ng</u>th, de<u>p</u>th, sho<u>r</u>e, stro<u>ng</u>, and Dut<u>ch</u>.

The construction *que* counts as a compound consonant and can be pronounced *kw,* as in *quench,* or *k,* as in *oblique.*

The *th* sound at the beginning or ends of words can be pronounced in two different ways: with a short *th*—*birth, death, myth, thin*—or a long *th*—*bequeath, betroth, booth, those.*

Shhhhh . . .

There is sometimes confusion as to whether to use the sound *s* or *sh* in certain words. For instance, *sociology* is often pronounced "so*sh*iology" instead of "so*s*iology." Both are acceptable, but *sh* is well on the way to supplanting the traditional *s*. Other words in which *sh* is taking over the simpler *s* sound are *associate, glacial,* and *negotiate.*

Emphasis

Emphasis plays a huge role in the English language. It is the key to pronunciation, to the rhythm of the sentence, and carries great persuasive power. It comes as no surprise, then, that it is impossible to arrive at any rules for the emphasizing of English words. Emphasis, or stress, can fall on any syllable, and often on more than one. It is difficult to enunciate more than three unstressed syllables, so there is a tendency in long words to push the stress toward the middle of the word, since a first-syllable stress might leave dangling too many unstressed syllables. But a more powerful tradition is to move the emphasis to the front of the word. Let's take it syllable by syllable.

Two-Syllable Words

These commonly place the stress on the first syllable—*master, other, standard, ticket.* When the stress falls on the second syllable, it is often to distinguish a verb from a noun—*rebel* (noun), *rebel* (verb)—or the retained pronunciation of an imported word—*lapel.* The stress distinction between verb and noun in two-syllable words is general but not absolute. Some nouns stress the second syllable, as in *dispute.*

Three-Syllable Words

Again the stress tends to be on the first syllable—*culminate, pimpernel*—and very rarely on the last. A few words place the stress on the second syllable—*conversant, pariah.*

Four-Syllable Words

This is where it gets interesting, because while the general tendency is to stress the word at the front, in some words the emphasis moves toward the middle to avoid mumbling too many unstressed syllables: *aristocrat, kilometer,* among many others. The "antepenultimate" stress is common, if not universal, in *centenary, despicable, hospitable, pejorative,* and, again, many others.

Five-Syllable Words

Take a word like *arbitrarily*. If you stress the first syllable, it is more or less impossible to get the rest out of your mouth in any comprehensible shape, except by eliding the *ari* and saying *arbitraly*. So the stress is placed on *arbitrarily*, and even then it's a bit of a mouthful. The word *veterinary* is interesting. We give each syllable its full due and place the emphasis twice, on *vet* and *in*. The British elide shamelessly and say something like *vetrinry*. Neither solution to the five-syllable problem is entirely satisfactory. British English elision gives *momentrily* for *momentarily*, while the American *momentarily*, though praiseworthy, is ponderous. Sometimes a long word—six syllables, in this case—pans out more happily, and a first-syllable stress can be supported by an "antepenultimate" stress—*incontrovertible*.

Punctuation

> "The writer who neglects punctuation, or mispunctuates,
> is liable to be misunderstood. . . . For the want of merely
> a comma, it often occurs that an axiom appears a paradox,
> or that a sarcasm is converted into a sermonoid."
> —EDGAR ALLAN POE

The word "punctuation" comes from the Latin *punctuare,* which means "to prick" or "to point," originally from *punctum,* "a point." There is a general rule when it comes to punctuating the English language: Do as little as possible. The reason for this is not only that overpunctuation clutters the page and frustrates the reader; it is also because punctuation *does* something, and if you overuse punctuation, it may entirely change the meaning of the same sequence of words.

Careful punctuation, on the other hand, can help to clarify writing by directing the reader to the author's intended meaning.

Weigh Your Options

A time-worn joke between a college professor and his students is possibly the best example of how punctuation can completely change the meaning of a sentence.

A college professor writes on his blackboard:

A woman without her man is nothing.

He then invites his students to punctuate this sentence. All the male students write:

A woman, without her man, is nothing.

All the female students write:

A woman: without her, man is nothing.

Look at the following sentences:

They opened fire with live ammunition.
They opened fire, with live ammunition!

The first is a statement of fact. The second, by creating a pause with the comma and weighting the end of the sentence with an exclamation point, invites or provokes an attitude. It could be one of shock or of indignation. It could conceivably be one of approval. But the punctuation divides the two sentences into two very different communications.

But to punctuate sparsely does not mean to punctuate

Punctuation Pointers

A very early form of punctuation was found in a work dating as far back as the ninth century B.C., when the ancient Greek dramatists were using a form of punctuation to guide the actors' speech. With the growth of education and the production of copies of the Bible and other holy works regularly read aloud or, in the case of plainsong, sung from, the scribes (or, indeed, scriveners) introduced marks to guide those singing or reciting such works.

As reading became more widespread, punctuation's role expanded to its modern purpose of guiding the mind in making sense of the written word, helping readers to "hear" the cadence and to therefore aid understanding.

casually. If you are going to use any of the 11 punctuation marks normally used in English, it is as essential to know why, when, and how to employ them. As with so much else concerned with English, there are few cast-iron rules but many indications and suggestions.

The Comma

Generally, the comma's function is to separate the grammatical components of a sentence with only the slightest pause of thought. It is not necessary to separate every phrase and clause from its neighbor with commas, but sometimes you will need to, because the comma, for all its small size, is a powerful thing. Consider the following sentence:

We sat happily on the terrace watching the sheep in the meadow holding hands and drinking wine.

Unless these are very versatile sheep, some punctuation is needed. The most economical solution is to place a comma after the word *meadow*. At all costs the sheep must be separated from the idea of holding hands. But a more profuse punctuator might add a second comma after *terrace* and a third after *hands*.

A comma, or commas, may be used in the following circumstances.

Wherever you wish your readers to pause for a moment. This is usually when a subordinate clause precedes a main clause, but it can be between any two clauses or phrases:

Whatever I have done, I am truly sorry for it.

"I think, therefore I am."
                    —René Descartes, *Discours de la Méthode*

After a short, nonessential introductory phrase or word that comes before the main clause of a sentence if it improves the flow:

Sentence Strategy

When in doubt about whether a comma is needed after an introductory phrase, count. If the introductory clause is five words or more, a comma will help reading. Shorter than five words, it's up to you.

Afterward, I changed my mind about his guilt.

Once upon a time, there lived a girl named Little Red Riding Hood.

Between the two main clauses joined by conjunctions, like *and, or, but*:

I like to sing, and he likes to dance.
He likes to dance, but I like to sing.

Before direct speech:

He said, "Where are my car keys?"

And in sequences of adjectives or adverbs. Normally you should use a comma between adjectives modifying the same noun, or adverbs modifying the same noun:

A low, furtive type.

If the second adjective is more "important"—more closely related to the noun—than the first, you omit the comma:

A furtive foreign type.

The comma is also omitted where the word *and* joins the adjectives:

A low and furtive type.

It should be inserted in lists of more than two nouns:

I met her mother, her best friend, and her personal trainer.

The comma before *and* is properly called the serial, or series, comma and is standard. Without the comma,

I met her mother, her best friend and her personal trainer.

This could mean that her mother is also her best friend and personal trainer.

To enclose any parenthetical clause or phrase, like the non-restrictive relative clauses discussed on page 62. That is, anything that might otherwise be put in brackets:

He picked up the book, which had been placed there by his secretary, and threw it at the wall with considerable force.

The children, who were of similar ages, were assigned to different classes.

In the second example, it is important to note that if the commas are dropped, the sentence has another meaning. As it stands, it means that certain children, who happen to be of similar ages, were assigned to different classes. If you remove the commas, it means that all children of a similar age were assigned to different classes.

A comma should also be used before and after what is called an appositive—a word or phrase that defines, or enlarges on, the word that immediately precedes it:

I, the undersigned, declare myself to be of sound mind.

We, the victims of this fraud, are taking legal action to recover our money.

To break up large numbers expressed in figures. When a number exceeds three digits, a comma is inserted at every third digit from the right:

1,000   *20,000*
300,000   *4,000,000*

With *although, but, for, however, like, moreover, so,* and *yet*:

He burst into tears, although he knew not why.

He stumbled blindly on, like a man lost in thought.

Moreover, if you think your mother will take a lenient view of this, you are mistaken, young man.

We've worked long enough, so let's take a break.

If a preposition is used in another form, a comma can be used to avoid misunderstanding:

In the valley below, the church bells were ringing.

The day after, the party ended.

Sentence Strategy

Don't use a comma:

- **Between the subject and the verb:** The dog, chased the cat and the mouse.
- **In compound phrases:** The dog chased the cat, and the mouse.
- **After a conjunction:** The dog chased the cat, and, the cat chased the mouse.

The Colons

The colon and the semicolon are not used as much as they used to be, or as systematically. In spite of sharing a name, they have very different functions.

The semicolon is a sort of souped-up comma, separating phrases, clauses, sentences, and complex items in lists and sequences. It often replaces conjunctions like *and* and *but*. The clauses it separates should be of roughly equal weight:

Religion comforts man; science advances him.

We tried to get to Milwaukee; the weather was against it.

When a semicolon joins two sentences, do not use a conjunction between them. The semicolon takes the place of the conjunction. It can also be used to break up lists in which the items are long and complicated:

*Expel International proudly proclaims that its
    corporate mission is to put the customer first;
    to drive down costs, raise productivity, and stay
    competitive; to provide better shareholder value;
    to care for its people; and to strive for excellence
    in every area of its activities.*

The colon breaks the rhythm of a sentence to introduce a description or example of what preceded the colon: a list detailing what has been mentioned in general, or another main clause amplifying the preceding clause. It can also be inserted to set off the elements within a set:

*I was delighted when I passed my math exam: It was
    my eighth attempt.*

*There were 33 of them: 11 Irishmen, 11 Scotsmen,
    and 11 Englishmen.*

The Period

The period is the most definitive punctuation mark. It's used to indicate a stop, such as the end of a sentence. Compared with the comma, its function is simple, but it is not the only mark that can bring closure to a sentence; the question mark and exclamation point share the same honor, depending on the tone.

Even the longest sentence must at last end:

"On this evening I was thinking these wholesome but not original thoughts and feeling extraordinarily virtuous because I had worked well and hard on a day when I had wanted to go out to the races very badly."
—Ernest Hemingway, *A Moveable Feast*

The period also closes abbreviations. If a sentence ends with an abbreviation, one period does both jobs.

Abbreviations that can be read as a word in their own right tend, through use, to cease to be abbreviations, and do without punctuation:

influenza = flu
telephone = phone
violoncello = cello

Use a period to end an abbreviation that finishes with a lowercase letter—*Mr., Dr., e.g., a.m.*—but it is not necessary to include a period with abbreviations that end with a capital letter, such as *PhD, BC, AD.* The initials of several words that, when run together, can be pronounced as a word are called an acronym—*AIDS, NATO, radar, scuba*—and are unpunctuated.

The Question Mark?

The question mark indicates an interrogative sentence:

> *"Where are the songs of spring? Ay, where are they?"*
> —John Keats, *Ode to Autumn*

The question mark can be used facetiously in brackets, or almost anywhere, to indicate disbelief:

Although she's only thirty-five (?), she's been married three times.

This is a slangy and informal usage. It's often better to use words to express your sarcasm.

A question mark should not be used after sentences that contain an implied question:

They asked me why I did not understand grammar.

In casual speech questions are often phrased as statements and given an interrogative cadence. In writing casual speech of this kind, you can use a question mark to stand in for the human voice:

You think I'm stupid or something?

The Exclamation Point!

Use it sparingly, certainly, but sometimes you really must use it. The rule is simple: You may use an exclamation point to mark an exclamation. Here are the four types of phrases and clauses that qualify as exclamations:

- interjections—*Oh! By Jove! Wow! Never!*
- phrases or clauses containing "what" or "how" in the exclamatory mood—*How I love you! What a whopper!*
- phrases or clauses in the optative mood (expressing a wish)—*God forbid! To hell with it!*
- ellipses and inversions that are done for emotional effect—*A fine friend you are! Like I care! Not another word!*

Sentence Strategy

A short word about interjections. Depending on the context, almost any single word or short phrase can be used as an interjection, and sometimes punctuation is needed to avoid confusion.

> *Bears! Please stay in your car.*
> *Sheep! Dogs must be on leashes.*
> *Slow! Lions with young.*

Strictly speaking, the words *bears, sheep,* and *slow* are not interjections, but here the exclamation points are justified for emphasis and to avoid confusion.

It is not essential to use an exclamation point with all these examples, but it should be noted that exclamations like "How I love you!" and "How we laughed!" are not complete without the exclamation point.

A straightforward sentence should not be given an exclamation point simply to add effect:

Be quiet immediately.   *I said go away.*
That's a lie.

The words themselves carry enough weight, and they are not, grammatically, exclamations.

The Apostrophe

An apostrophe looks like a raised comma and causes a great deal of confusion. It originates in the Greek rhetorical device *apostrephein,* in which the speaker addressed not the audience but some absent thing or person. It now indicates something that is missing, usually letters. Below are three of its most basic uses.

1. An apostrophe can indicate possession:

- In normal singular words—*a baker's dozen, a dog's dinner, his master's voice*
- in singular words ending in *s*—*Corporal Jones's bayonet, St. James's Street*
- in plural possessives not ending in *s*—*the people's flag, policemen's ball*

- in plural possessives that end in s—*birds' nests, the dogs' kennels*—you don't need to add an extra s, because the apostrophe does the job on its own
- It is not used in the possessive pronouns—*hers, his, its*

Sentence Strategy

It's *vs.* Its

It's = It is

Its = possessive

It's sometimes tricky to know when it's right to use its different forms.

---

2. It can be used to mark a contraction:

- *o'clock (of the clock), she'll (she will), wouldn't (would not), you're (you are)*

3. And only very, very, very occasionally, an apostrophe can mark plurals that would be confusing if left unmarked:

- *Dot your i's and cross your t's.*

This is a dangerous one. Normally, you do not use an apostrophe plus s to make a plural. But when dealing with letters of the alphabet, it's best to insert the apostrophe to avoid forming new words. When in doubt, leave it out and see how it looks. But best to err on the side of caution.

"Quotation Marks"

Quotation marks enclose direct speech. They are also used to indicate quotations, to distinguish titles of shorter publications, and occasionally to suggest irony. They can cause confusion where quoted speech falls within direct speech, and where direct speech or a quotation falls at the end of a sentence.

Double quotation marks set off direct quotations, and single quotation marks enclose a quotation within a quotation.

He said, "I distinctly heard her say, 'You're both invited.' "

This brings us to a second bone of contention. Where should the period go at the end of a sentence with quoted speech in it?

Generally speaking, commas and periods go inside the quotation marks, but colons and semicolons are set outside. Dashes, question marks, and exclamation points go inside the quotation marks only if they're part of the quotation.

He told me to "pull the other handle."

I can't believe he told me to "pull the other handle"!

He shouted, "Pull the other handle!"

If you put the exclamation point inside the quotation marks, you're changing the quoted matter into an exclamation; if it's outside, then the whole sentence becomes exclamatory. Please note that you don't need a period if the quotation ends the sentence with an exclamation point or a question mark.

Quotation marks are used for the titles of articles or chapters in magazines or books, while the titles of the lengthier works are usually given in italic type. (If the text is already in italic, what is usually italicized is put in roman type.)

When I was at school, I knew Keats's "Ode to a Nightingale" by heart.

In The National Geographic *there is a fascinating article, "Spirits in the Sand."*

Quotation marks are also sometimes used like this to show that a term has a special meaning:

The trouble with "intellectuals" is that they are so impractical.

The quotation marks clearly indicate that the writer is throwing doubt on their intelligence. This is a heavy-handed use of sarcasm and a bit cowardly—if you don't like intellectuals, say so.

([Parentheses and Brackets])

Parentheses, like commas and dashes, can be used to separate or fence off additional, not immediately relevant, material.

Square brackets are used to insert explanatory material by someone other than the author into a passage:

"However advantageous the peace, the war [the Crimean War of 1854] had been disastrously mishandled."

"Reader, I married him [Mr Rochester]."

Parentheses enclose subsidiary comments by the author:

Left to his own devices (and who can say what they might be?) he will get the job done satisfactorily.

Note that the surrounding punctuation is not affected by the use of parentheses.

Parentheses or brackets can sometimes occur within brackets:

(The Vagrancy [Prevention of] Act, 1894, 5. (2) and (6))

The possible confusion at the end of the parenthesis is solved typographically, by leaving a space between the identical closing brackets. Official and legal documents can truly tie themselves in knots with constructions like this, which don't really fall within the sphere of a discussion of English, being more a form of religious incantation.

Square brackets might also be used for parenthetical matter within a parenthesis:

He told us to choose something to read (I chose **The Mill on the Floss** *by George Eliot [a famous Victorian woman novelist]) and said he'd be back in an hour.*

The Hy-phen

A hyphen is a short dash used to join two or more words to emphasize the closeness of their relationship. Hyphens joining two words into a compound tend to disappear with use, as the words they join merge into one: There's no more hyphen in crossword, for example.

But in some contexts they are essential:

Twelve-year-old boys cannot be expected to undertake the rigors of a long hike with loaded backpacks.

If you omit one of the hyphens, they certainly cannot:

Twelve year-old boys cannot be expected to undertake the rigors of a long hike with loaded backpacks.

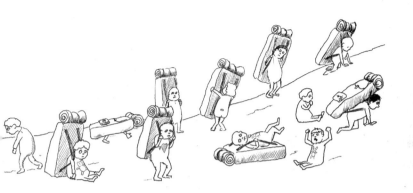

Bach wrote 200-odd cantatas.

Nothing odd about them at all.

Hyphens are traditionally used to join two words to act as a single modifier:

a ten-ton truck
a twelve-mile run
a three-course meal

These are often omitted, even in print, and usually the meaning is clear from the rest of the text—but it is better to remain clear and consistent and use them.

Hyphens are also used to divide words at the end of lines. Your word-processing program probably does this for you, but it's useful to know a few simple rules. Always break words between syllables—*pan-cakes or ba-con*—but never divide a one-syllable word, like eggs. If you're not sure where to break a word, check a dictionary.

The Dash—

As well as the hyphen, English typography uses two other dashes: the *en* dash, a line slightly longer than the hyphen, and the *em* dash, which is generally twice the length of the *en*. Their lengths vary with the typeface and type size, and—as you might have guessed—they were based on the captial *M* and lowercase *n* in the days when printing used a metal block to represent every character.

The *en* rule is used typographically to connect numbers or to join pairs of words or phrases:

1984–1988
the Kennedy–Nixon debate

The dash is used in place of other punctuation—commas, parentheses, or colons:

I said I hadn't seen her—and he believed me.

I said I hadn't seen her—it was true, after all—and he believed me.

It indicates an interruption of some kind, such as a change in tone or idea, or it can set off nonessential elements.

Or it can indicate that a sentence has been broken off:

We like the idea, but—

Although dashes are undeniably useful, overuse can appear sloppy and can irritate the reader. Be sparing.

Clear Usage

> "The end of speech is not ostentation, but to be understood." —WILLIAM PENN

If you have read this far, you will be used to the refrain "There are no rules." There are certainly no clear rules about what is "good" English and what is "bad." Fashion plays too great a part in such judgments, and many other influences ceaselessly transform language from one generation to the next.

But there are very helpful guidelines for writing simple, concise, and clear prose, a more difficult exercise than is commonly thought. There are, of course, wide differences between formal speech and writing and casual speech.

All the departures from clear English listed below—and indeed all errors of vocabulary and grammar—can be used with effect if you are trying to be amusing. But "trying," perhaps, is the important word.

"Do not put statements in the negative form.
And don't start sentences with a conjunction.
If you reread your work, you will find on rereading
*   that a great deal of repetition can be avoided by*
*   rereading and editing.*
Never use a long word when a diminutive one will do.
Unqualified superlatives are the worst of all.
De-accession euphemisms.
If any word is improper at the end of a sentence, a
*   linking verb is.*
Avoid trendy locutions that sound flaky.
Last, but not least, avoid cliches like the plague."

—William Safire, *Great Rules of Writing*

Sincerity

"The great enemy of clear language is insincerity.
When there is a gap between one's real and one's declared
aims, one turns as it were instinctively to long words
and exhausted idioms, like a cuttlefish squirting out ink."
—GEORGE ORWELL, *POLITICS AND THE ENGLISH LANGUAGE*

George Orwell's point is more moral than grammatical, but it is worth making all the same. If you try to use language to conceal rather than reveal, or to deceive rather than inform, it becomes difficult to express yourself clearly. The hyperbole of advertisers and the evasive rigmarole of politicians are more than adequate illustrations of this point.

"Oil and coal? Of course, it's a fungible commodity and they don't flag, you know, the molecules, where it's going and where it's not. But in the sense of the Congress today, they know that there are very, very hungry domestic markets that need that oil first. So, I believe that what Congress is going to do, also, is not to allow the export bans to such a degree that it's Americans that get stuck to holding the bag without the energy source that is produced here, pumped here. It's got to flow into our domestic markets first."

—Sarah Palin, speaking off the cuff
at a town hall meeting in Grand Rapids,
Michigan, September 17, 2008

Don't Use No Double Negatives

Logically, two negatives make a positive. From that point of view, the utterance "I don't have nothing" means that you do have something. Double negatives can be used ironically—the example just given, for example, could be used ironically by a very rich man. In the same way "He's not unattractive" could be used as a kind way of saying that in reality he's just average, or as an unkind way of avoiding having to say that, actually, he's great-looking. The sense would depend on context, manner, and tone.

The conscious use of double negatives can become an annoying affectation. It overcomplicates your sentences and often baffles the reader. In formal speech and writing, double negatives should be avoided. It's easy to cure yourself. As George Orwell suggested, memorize the following sentence:

*A **not unblack** dog was chasing a **not unsmall** rabbit across a **not ungreen** field.*

In speech, however, it's a different matter. Double—and even triple and quadruple—negatives abound, and the listener would have to be very obtuse not to understand them. Their main purpose is emphasis:

I won't give up, not now, not never.

And a neat foursome from the great Satchmo himself:

"All music is folk music. I ain't never heard no horse sing no song." —Louis Armstrong

Armstrong makes himself a great deal clearer than the following:

"I am not, indeed, sure whether it is not true to say that the Milton who once seemed not unlike a seventeenth-century Shelley had not become, out of an experience even more bitter in each year, more alien to the founder of that Jesuit sect which nothing would induce him to tolerate."
                    —Harold Laski, *Essay in Freedom of Expression*

Ties himself in nots, you might say.

Pretentious? *Moi?*

The overuse of foreign words—or even any use of foreign words—where perfectly good English alternatives exist is merely a form of showing off your learning. And you better be sure that your learning is correct.

"Perfume is a subject dear to my heart. I have so many favorites: Arome de Grenouille, Okefenokee, Eau Contraire, Fume de ma Tante, Blast du Past, Kermes, Je Suis Swell, and Attention S'il Vous Plaît, to name but a few." —Miss Piggy's Guide to Life

The tendency of English to borrow foreign words without changing their form can lead to confusion. It is not pretentious to use words like *negligee* or *tête-à-tête,* because (a) they have entered English as normal words (*negligee* so much so that it has dropped its accents), and (b) there is no concise English alternative. But words or phrases like *bêtise, distrait, nom de plume,* or *Schadenfreude* have perfectly good English alternatives—stupidity, absent-minded, pen name, and malicious pleasure. To load your conversation and writing with these and many other popular foreign words is pretentious—until they become so widespread that you gain no kudos (credit, fame, renown, prestige) by using them.

Diplomats are grave offenders in this respect and, in the hurly-burly of international intrigue, scramble whole squadrons of foreign words to shoot down their opponents—*détente, rapprochement,* and many others. Unless it is your perverse wish to be mistaken for a diplomat, avoid these words.

The situation about foreign words is certainly confusing. So many words have been drafted into English that the best general rule is to ask yourself: Which word will be understood by more people? You will be understood by more people if you use the word *anemone* in preference to *wind flower.* On the other hand, more people will understand *snapdragon* than will understand *antirrhinum.*

Happy are they who speak foreign languages so well that they know instantly what foreign words mean. Happier still are they who speak no foreign language at all and are free from temptation.

Concrete or Abstract?

The overuse of abstract nouns and phrases clogs up sentences and confuses their meaning. An abstract word denotes a quality or an idea, while a concrete word denotes a thing. The word *telephone* is concrete. We can all picture a telephone or experience the act of telephoning. *Telephonic* is abstract. It is far better to say "I called her on the telephone" than to say "I was in telephonic communication with her." Because *telephonic* is abstract, it needs other long words to help it along, causing you to end up with an unnecessarily long sentence.

> *"A **writer** uses abstract words because his thoughts are cloudy; the habit of using them clouds his thoughts still further; he may end by concealing his meaning not only from his readers but also from himself."* —Henry Fowler, *Modern English Usage*

Anyone who doubts the accuracy of this prophecy has only to read a sentence or two of many academic writings.

Here are more abstractions, along with their concrete alternatives:

*A **cessation of hostilities was negotiated**.* (**They agreed to stop fighting.**)

*Oil **resources are diminishing**.* (**There is less oil.**)

*Participation by the **workforce** in the **management process** is a top priority.* (**We want workers to take part in management.**)

Swathes of people in business, government, and academia succumb to the temptation to think and write like this. Concrete writing exposes your thinking to inspection, and it may not withstand inspection. Much safer to hide behind abstractions.

The use of abstractions is closely linked to periphrasis, or the deliberate phrasing of simple ideas in a roundabout and awkward way. Periphrasis is often an attempt at humor. *The answer is in the affirmative* is a periphrasis for *yes. My feline companion* is a periphrasis for *my cat.* Both periphrasis and abstraction overlap with the vice of wordiness, and all three should be avoided.

Wordiness, or How to Avoid Using Too Many Words to Say Not Very Much

Also called pleonasm, long-windedness, verbosity, prolixity, and logorrhoea, wordiness is the fault of using more words than necessary to express your meaning—sometimes many more words than necessary:

"It [the red kite] is, nevertheless, a bird well-known, partly on account of its peculiar flight and appearance, which render it easily distinguishable from all other predaceous birds; and still more, perhaps, on account of its habits, which render it peculiarly obnoxious to man, from its partiality for the young of various species of game, as well as for the cherished nurslings of the farmyard."

—H. L. Meyer, *British Birds and Their Eggs*

Victorian ornithologists appear to have been especially prone to logorrhoea:

"The vernacular name of this bird [the nuthatch], as descriptive of its habit of hacking and hewing at the nuts, which furnish it with food, is derived from some primitive word, the original likewise of the word hatchet, as is its second name of Nutjobber, from another root of like import."
—The Rev. F. O. Morris, *A History of British Birds*

The first extract, by H. L. Meyer, could read "The red kite is easily recognizable and does much damage by killing young game birds and chickens." I shall not even attempt to paraphrase the Rev. F. O. Morris.

Tautology

Tautology, saying the same thing twice, is wordiness on a smaller scale but of greater grammatical importance. saying the same thing twice. It is easy to fall into this error by using—for the purposes of emphasis—two or more words that give the same meaning:

a round ball   *lend out*
adequate enough   *meet with*
raze to the ground   *collaborate together*
refer back   *continue on*
gather together   *rise up*
sink down   *final completion*
twice over   *follow after*
join together   *young child*

So much of casual speech is tautological that it is very difficult to avoid falling into this trap in speech, although in writing, the effort should be made to avoid it. Some writers should be above suspicion:

"All public information should be crystal clear."
—Plain English Charter, Plain English Campaign website

The redundant *crystal clear* is then repeated three times in the same document.

Steer Clear of Clichés and Tired Phrases

To qualify as a cliché, a word or phrase must be two things. It must be commonplace to start with, and it must be thoroughly overused— indiscriminately and unsuitably overused—  until it no longer communicates any precise meaning but just a general feeling. There are many stereotyped phrases that retain some meaning and can still be used to some purpose—*blessing in disguise, foregone conclusion, tongue in cheek.*

But the list of "dead" ready-made words and phrases is long. Most are still in daily use and do nothing to illuminate the reader or listener. Only a very few examples can be given here:

acid test	*aid and abet*
ill-gotten gains	*all manner of*
of that ilk	*at the end of the day*
powers that be	*bottom line*
tender mercies	*level playing field*
tower of strength	*fair sex*

When a word or phrase pops too readily into your mind, examine it carefully. When in doubt, avoid the usual suspects.

Anglo-Saxon or Latin?

It is a general rule of English that Anglo-Saxon root words are preferable to Latin root words, being usually shorter and more concrete. But this is not an absolute rule. As someone wittily observed, "Why should 'the un-go-throughsomeness of stuff' be better than 'the impenetrability of matter'?" It would also be difficult to decide between *betterment* and *improvement,* or between *happenings* and *events.* Since about a third of the English vocabulary consists of Latin root words, it would be a great waste to discard even a minority of them. Where the rule comes in useful is where it discourages circumlocution:

The contest was abandoned due to adverse climatic conditions. (Rain stopped play.)

Financial malpractice is a global phenomenon. (Cheating is worldwide.)

Active or Passive?

Avoid the passive voice where possible. Constructions like *it is thought that* and *it was believed that* leave open the questions "Who thought?" and "Who believed?" As a result they sound vague, imprecise, and even a bit shifty.

In straightforward sentences the active voice always sounds clearer: *I will help you* is clearer than *You will be helped by me.* The passive comes into its own when the knowledge behind the sentence is incomplete. *You will be helped* is one way of putting it if the helper is not known (*Someone will help you* is the active alternative).

The passive voice is tempting when you want to avoid responsibility. *The entire workforce was fired* is a more comforting way of saying, *I fired them all.* The passive gets especially cumbersome in a double construction. So, *He is believed to have been abducted by terrorists* should read *Most believe that terrorists abducted him.*

Pitfalls and Confusions

This chapter lists alphabetically the more frequent misunderstandings that English gives rise to. Most of them are pairs of words whose similar spelling, sound, or meaning causes confusion. Some are here simply because they have always confused me.

Abuse/misuse To abuse someone is either to attack him with harsh language or to mistreat him. The dictionary definitions of abuse stress wrong use rather than ill usage, but in tabloid journalism, abuse almost always implies sexual maltreatment. To misuse is milder and means merely to use ineptly or to do minor harm. The word disabuse means to correct a wrong impression: *I was quickly disabused of the idea that English is easy to learn.*

Accurate/precise These two words do not mean the same thing. If a bird-watcher exclaims, *"There's a flock of finches!"* he is being accurate (assuming for the moment that they are finches). But if he says, *"There's a flock of* Fringilla coelebs, *or, as I like to call them, chaffinches!"* he is being precise. You can be accurate without being precise, but you can't be precise without being accurate.

Affect/effect Usually, affect is used as a verb and effect as a noun, but each can be used as both. To affect something is (a) to influence it or (b) to pretend to it: *This will affect the outcome* or *He affected a Boston accent.* To effect something is to accomplish it: *They effected an entry.* Effect is also the noun related to affect—as in *The law affected nobody/The law had no effect on anybody.* Effects as a plural noun also means possessions, as in *personal effects.* Affect as a noun is a psychological term to describe a feeling or emotion.

Affront/effrontery An affront is an insult: *The doctrine of Intelligent Design is an affront to the intelligence.* Effrontery is a general mood of insolence and impertinence: *He has the effrontery to suggest that the doctrine of Intelligent Design is unintelligent.*

All together/altogether All together means as one, while altogether means completely:

It was a pleasant change for the family to be all together at Christmas.

We were not altogether happy to be in Montana for the holiday.

Alternate/alternative. As a verb, alternate means to happen by turns. As an adjective, happening by turns. As an adjective, it is not a synonym for alternative. You cannot say *I have an alternate solution* nor should you be able to say *I have an alternative solution* unless you have only two solutions, because, strictly speaking, an alternative can be one of only two options. But it is used so freely to mean one of any number of options that it is petty to object, and this general use is now acceptable. Alternative is also used as a label for any activity undertaken to flout the general custom—*alternative lifestyle, alternative medicine.*

You should ask yourself, "Alternative to what?"

Amend/emend *Amend* is to improve something for the better: *Will he ever amend his wretched ways?* Emend is to correct written errors: *I attach the emended manuscript.*

Amiable/amicable Both mean friendly. Amiable refers to human beings, and sometimes animals or (rarely) events: *an amiable fellow, an amiable dog, an amiable conversation.* Amicable is used only of human relationships: *an amicable discussion, an amicable settlement.*

Amoral/immoral Amoral means not concerned whether something is right or wrong, nonmoral. Immoral means not conforming to or opposed to accepted standards of morality, unprincipled.

Antimony/antinomy Antimony is a hard metallic substance, while antinomy is a conflict of authority or a contradiction in law.

Appraise/apprise To appraise is to weigh up or judge: *He appraised the situation.* To apprise is to inform: *He apprised me of the situation.*

Assignation/assignment An assignation is an arranged meeting—almost always a meeting to pursue a secret liaison—while an assignment is a task given (assigned) to you by someone else. One of life's tragedies is that one is never assigned an assignation.

Assume/presume In their shared meaning of suppose, these words have subtly different implications. You assume something—that is, you take it to be the case—without any evidence, because it seems to be likely: *I assume you'll be coming on Tuesday.* But you presume something on much stronger grounds—when there's no good reason to think otherwise: *"Dr. Livingstone, I presume?"* Henry Stanley was quite right to presume. It wasn't going to be the King of Siam, was it?

Bacteria/bacterium Bacteria is always a plural, so should never be given a singular verb. *The smallpox bacteria is highly infectious* is incorrect; that sentence should start *The smallpox bacterium . . .*

Beg the question To beg the question is to argue in a circle by assuming at the outset that what you want to prove is true. The phrase is a somewhat ambiguous translation of the Latin *petitio principii,* which might more helpfully be translated as "assuming the initial point." Properly, therefore, it refers to a particular, logically unsustainable method of argument.

It is also widely used—incorrectly—to mean "evade the question" and "raise the question." Along with many other slipshod usages, these two meanings are gaining ground and will no doubt supplant the correct meaning in due course. It is idle to point out that the two corrupt meanings do not mean the same thing and are as much at odds with each other as with the original.

Beside/besides Beside means next to, while besides means in addition to or as well as.

Biannual/biennial Biannual means twice yearly; biennial means every two years.

Billion In both the United States and Britain, a million is a thousand thousand. In American usage, a billion is one thousand million. In British usage, it means one million million. A difference of this magnitude could give rise to very expensive mistakes, and both business and the sciences have adopted the American usage. The English system progresses in multiples of a million: a billion is a million squared; a trillion, a million cubed; a quadrillion, a million to the power of four. The American system proceeds by the power of a thousand at each stage: a million is a thousand squared; a billion, a thousand cubed; a trillion, a thousand to the power of four—and so on. The American system is easier and gives rich people an inflated impression of their wealth. It is becoming universal.

Carousal/carousel A carousal is a drunken celebration, while a carousel is a merry-go-round at the amusement park and, by extension, the conveyor system that delivers luggage at an airport.

Casual/causal Casual means informal or lackadaisical, while causal means relating to or acting as a cause.

Censor/censure To censor is to forbid publication: *The government has censored all news coming out of the occupied zone.* To censure is to criticize severely, often officially: *Nurses at the hospital were censured for organizing a poker school in the ICU.*

Childish/childlike Both mean pertaining to childhood, but with a difference. Childish is used in a pejorative sense of an adult behaving like a child. Childlike is used with approval to suggest the innocence of childhood.

Chronic Used colloquially to mean merely "very bad"—*her lumbago is something chronic*—chronic means long-lasting, as in *chronic shortages* and *chronic unemployment*. Medically it means a long-lasting disease, as opposed to a swift-acting disease, which is "acute."

Climactic/climatic Climactic is the adjective from climax, as in *climactic moment*. Climatic refers to the climate, as in *climatic conditions*.

Compare/contrast Generally, you compare something *with* something else and contrast a thing to another thing.

You may, however, sometimes use "compare to"—*Shall I compare thee to a summer's day?*—when you are emphasizing the similarities of the things compared rather than their dissimilarities. Use contrast when you are focusing on differences.

Complacent/complaisant If you're complacent, you're pleased with yourself, or smug. If you're complaisant, you are anxious to please, or obliging. *She was complacent about having known so many complaisant men.*

Complement/compliment A complement is something that completes: *That tie complements your shirt*—that is, it makes the appearance complete. A complement completes the otherwise incomplete copulative verbs (see page 67). A ship's complement is the full number of sailors required to sail it. A compliment, on the other hand, is a flattering address: *You look lovely today, darling.*

Comprehensible/comprehensive Comprehensible means understandable, while comprehensive means exhaustive, complete, covering the whole waterfront. *Her clear tones were entirely comprehensible, and her searching analysis of my shortcomings was comprehensive.*

Comprise The verb "to comprise" means "to consist of." It doesn't need an extra "of." It does not mean "include" or "contain" or "constitute." These are the correct distinctions:

A baseball team comprises nine players.
A baseball team consists of nine players.
A baseball team includes a pitcher.
A baseball team contains three basemen.
Nine players constitute a baseball team.

The verb "to comprise" can appear only in the first of these examples. In all the other positions—where it is frequently found in many similar constructions—it is incorrect.

Connote/denote To connote is to imply something more than the basic meaning of a word: *The word "nature" has many connotations.* To denote is to indicate or signify: *The company he chooses denotes the man who boozes.*

Creole/pidgin Creole is a mother tongue, a fully developed language, often originating in a pidgin language, with complex grammar and a large vocabulary. A pidgin language is an extemporized, incomplete language, lacking sophistication, which develops when two groups with no common tongue meet. It is not a mother tongue.

Cynic/skeptic A cynic is one who takes an unrelentingly dim view of people, events, institutions, and the world in general; one who always thinks the worst. A skeptic (not to be confused with septic, or infected) is one who doubts until his doubts can be resolved by evidence.

Data The word data is a plural, uncountable noun, but it would be fussy to insist that it always take a plural verb.

The computer sciences have more or less hijacked this word, and they use it as a collective noun, which, as we know, may take either a singular or a plural verb.

Decorative/decorous It is difficult, but not impossible, to be both decorative and decorous. Decorative means attractive, good to look at. Decorous means having propriety in outward appearance and conduct.

Delusion/illusion To suffer from a delusion is to be seriously, fundamentally wrong. You are deluded if you believe the Earth is flat. Or you may have delusions of grandeur and think yourself entitled to a ten-gun salute. To suffer from an illusion, or to have illusions, is a much less serious affliction. An illusion may just be an accidental wrong impression, like an optical illusion. It is not difficult to cure an illusion and become disillusioned. You cannot become "disdelusioned"—at least not without extensive therapy or perhaps even a frontal lobotomy.

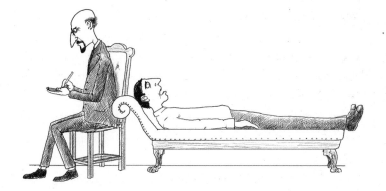

Deprecate/depreciate To deprecate means to express disapproval, while to depreciate means (a) to reduce in value or (b) to disparage.

The depreciation of the dollar will certainly help exports.
He resented the fact that they depreciated his efforts.
We deprecate this rash and ill-considered policy.

Derisive/derisory Derisive is mocking: *Derisive hoots greeted my efforts.* Derisory is contemptible: *Such derisory efforts will get you nowhere.*

Dialectal/dialectical Easily confused, but oh, how different. Dialectal means to do with dialects or concerning regional patterns of speech. All good, clean innocent fun. But dialectical means concerned with the rules and methods of reasoning.

Different "Different from" is normal and preferable. "Different to" is permissible in casual speech and writing. A simple memory aid—"different from": from suggests divergence as in "away from"; "similar to" brings the two, whatever they may be, closer to each other.

Discomfit/discomfort To discomfit means to thwart or embarrass—almost to humiliate: *Picture his discomfiture when he was publicly exposed as a fraud.* Discomfort means lack of ease, well-being, or contentment.

Discreet/discrete Discreet means tactful, reserved, not given to tittle-tattle:

"This child is dainty as the Cat,
And as the Owl discreet"—Hilaire Belloc

Discrete means separate, forming one unit, distinct: *The watertight compartments formed a series of discrete units.*

Discriminating/discriminatory If I discriminate between wines, pictures, types of Chinese porcelain, I am discriminating. If I discriminate *against* certain groups of people, I am discriminatory.

Disinterested/uninterested The difference between these two words reflects two meanings of the word *interest*. Disinterested means lacking interest in the sense of stake or share—in other words fair, impartial: *I care nothing for either side. I am a disinterested observer.* Uninterested means lacking interest in the sense of intellectual curiosity: *I care nothing for either team. I am uninterested in the result.*

Dissatisfied/unsatisfied When you are dissatisfied, you are discontent: *I was dissatisfied by the outcome of my exams.* When you are unsatisfied, some need remains unfulfilled: *The meager rations left me unsatisfied.*

Egoism/egotism Egoism was once the philosophical doctrine that we have no proof of anything beyond our own existence, while egotism was about being self-centered. Sigmund Freud applied special meanings to the ego and the superego, which it would seem sensible to reserve for the use of his disciples. But no. Ego and all its derivatives now refer to anything to do with self-importance.

Elemental/elementary Elemental means concerned with the elements—fire, storms, water, earth, air, and so on. Elementary means basic, concerned with first principles.

Enormity Universally used to mean an excess of size—which it does not. Correctly it means an excess of wickedness.

*He was appalled at the enormity of what he had
  done* (right).
We are proud of the enormity of our achievement
  (wrong, but funny).

The correct use of this word is probably beyond rescue.

Epigram/epigraph/epitaph/epithet An epigram is a witty remark like Oscar Wilde's *Work is the curse of the drinking classes.* An epigraph is a brief inscription, sometimes on a building or monument, sometimes in a book as a heading. An epitaph is a similar inscription, but always on a tombstone, or in some other way celebrating the dead. An epithet is a short descriptive statement, often applied to a person—*the charming but infuriating Chloe, smelly old Bill, Richard the Lionheart*.

Equality/equity Equality means having equal status. In legal and financial terms, equity can mean the balance or the residue. In general speech, it means fairness and is sometimes mistakenly used instead of equality.

Erotic/esoteric/exotic Erotic means amatory or designed to stimulate lust. It is sometimes confused with exotic, which means foreign or from another country, but has come to mean colorfully unusual. Esoteric—which means known only to the few—is a pretty innocent word, but there's no reason why really exotic erotica should not also be esoteric.

Euphemism/euphuism A euphemism is a way of evading an offensive or embarrassing word. "Downsizing" is a euphemism for firing someone. Modern English teems with this sort of mealy-mouthed evasion. Euphuism is an exaggerated, ornate style of writing, and possibly euphemism as well.

Evoke/invoke To evoke is to awaken a thought in the mind: *The smell of dust wetted by rain evokes memories of childhood.* To invoke is to call upon some source of help, or to cite a proof or an authority: *He invoked the authority of his position to justify his attitude.*

Facility/faculty Facility means ease in doing something: *He had an extraordinary facility for figures.* It is now generally used to mean amenities or services—*there is an in-house*

catering facility—a hideous and ignorant usage, but now unstoppable. The word shouldn't be confused with faculty, which means an inborn ability, like hearing and speech.

Factitious/fictitious Factitious means unnatural or artificial: *The plots of most operas are thoroughly factitious.* Fictitious means feigned or untrue: *His version of events was entirely fictitious.* The plots of most operas are also, of course, fictional, but that isn't the same as fictitious. Fictional merely means having to do with fiction, while fictitious definitely implies intending to deceive.

Foregoing/forgo The prefixes *fore-* and *for-* are easily confused. *Fore-* refers to time: foregoing = going before. *For-* as a prefix has many meanings, but here carries the sense of "without": forgo = do without. In the same way we get "forewarn" and "forbear." The rule is not consistent. "Forward" should have an *e,* and "therefore" should not.

Historic/historical Historic means memorable in the sense of making history, while historical means having taken place.

Hoi polloi Don't allow know-it-alls to tell you that because *hoi* means "the" in Greek, you can't say "the *hoi polloi.*" You can—if you don't mind sounding snobbish in a 1950s sort of way.

Homogeneous/homogenous Homogeneous means having the same composition, while homogenous means similar as a result of shared (evolutionary) descent. The backbones of vertebrates are homogenous structures. A uniformly blended chocolate milk would be homogeneous.

Hopefully Hopefully means with hope, not "I hope." Do not use the construction *Hopefully I will be there next week.* Say, *I hope I will be there next week.* You may say, however, *To travel hopefully is better than to arrive.*

Immanent/imminent Immanent means inherent in or pervading throughout, while imminent means immediately impending or about to happen, as in *his imminent arrival.*

Imply/infer To imply something is to insinuate it, to suggest it indirectly, while to infer something is to deduce it logically from facts and evidence: *He implied that I had stolen his book, and from this I inferred that he was too cowardly to accuse me outright.*

Inapt/inept Inapt is inappropriate or unsuitable, while inept is unskillful or clumsy: *It was inept of me to make such an inapt remark.* Their meanings can shade into each other very easily, but it is useful to maintain the distinction.

Incredible/incredulous Incredible means unbelievable, while incredulous means unbelieving. Even the sharpest mind can be at fault here.

Innovative Listen carefully to the speech of politicians, businessmen, radio and TV announcers, and many others and you will hear them use *innovative* to mean simply new. It means innovating or making changes.

Judicial/judicious The judicial system is the administration of the law. A judicial separation is a separation sanctioned or authorized by the law. Judicial means concerned with the law. A piece of judicious advice, however, is merely careful or well considered.

Literally Literal means not figurative or metaphorical, but actual, factual, and according to the letter, not the spirit, of the law. Literally is widely used as a general intensifier—*It's literally millions of miles away; I'm literally going mad over this*—often in contexts that are literally meaningless.

Lustful/lusty It would certainly help to be lusty if you were feeling lustful, but they mean different things. Lusty means vigorous and full of health, while lustful means anxious to procreate.

Masterful/masterly If you can command silence with a glance, you are masterful; you have a domineering or authoritative character. Masterly means in the manner of a master. You display masterly characteristics if you do something supremely well. You could of course be masterful and masterly—and unbearable.

Maximize/minimize Maximize means to make as great as possible, while minimize is to make as small as possible. There are no shades of meaning. You can't partly maximize or slightly minimize. Maximize should not be used simply to mean "make good" or "make the best of."

Militate/mitigate Militate is usually coupled with "against" and means to tell against or weigh against: *His record of* *unreliability will militate against his chances of success.* Mitigate means to lessen or alleviate: *A kindly twinkle in his eye mitigated the severity of his remarks.*

Mutual Reciprocal, not common or shared. The distinction is important enough to be worth retaining. Two people who love each other enjoy a mutual love. They may also both love animals, but they don't have a mutual love of animals, only a shared love of animals.

Naturalist/naturist A naturalist is one who exposes the living world to examination, while a naturist is one who exposes his body to the living world—a nudist.

Oblivious Oblivious used to mean only forgetful. You were therefore oblivious (forgetful) of something. American English has always used oblivious to, and oblivious itself has evolved to mean unaware or unconscious.

Obscene Excessively indecent in a sexual sense. It does not mean simply shocking or outrageous. *Bankers' salaries are obscenely inflated* is an incorrect usage—unless there are further and startling revelations to be made about pay in the financial services sector.

Optimal/optimum Optimal is the state in which conditions are at their most desirable or efficient, while the optimum is the point at which all conditions are at their most favorable. Mathematicians use both terms in a specialized sense. It is overblown to use either word as a general synonym for best.

Parricide/patricide Parricide is the killing of any near relative, especially a parent. Patricide is killing one's father, so it is also parricide.

Persecute/prosecute To persecute is systematically to oppress an individual or a group: *the persecution of the Roma*. Prosecute has a general meaning of to carry forward, as in *to prosecute a war,* but it usually means to bring to legal account: *Trespassers will be prosecuted.*

Perspicacious/perspicuous Perspicacious is showing insight or understanding, while perspicuous is lucid or easily understood.

Precede/proceed If one event precedes another, it goes before it. To proceed is to continue or carry on. Hence also proceedings—the operations of some group or undertaking: *The proceedings were preceded by a brief prayer meeting.*

Precipitate/precipitous To be precipitate is to be hasty or rash: *He made a precipitate departure on hearing that the police had been called.* Precipitous is having (near-vertical) steepness or being like a precipice: *The descent is precipitous, and not for those given to vertigo.*

Prescribe/proscribe To prescribe is to recommend or strongly advocate, while to proscribe is to forbid: *The doctor prescribed a light diet and exercise, but proscribed alcohol.*

Principal/principle Principal means most important or chief: *The principal of the school asserted that the prime consideration must always be the well-being of the child.* A principle is a rule or a moral scruple: *The principal of the school stated this his principle is always be the well-being of the child; Her principles would not allow her to eat meat.*

Pure "Pure spring water" may be pure water, although this is unlikely, but not because it is spring water. Pure does not mean natural. It means uncontaminated or unmixed with any other matter. Many claims to purity are made, especially in the food and drink industries. Ignore them.

Quantum leap Widely used outside its specialized use in physics to mean any big or sudden change: *There has been a quantum leap in the divorce rate.* In fact, quantum leap refers to the behavior of particles, which seem to be able to move from point to point without ever being "between" the points. Furthermore, the move is infinitesimally tiny by everyday standards. Borrowing terms from the sciences—especially physics—is even more risky than borrowing foreign words and terms.

Regretfully/regrettably Regretfully means with regret or in a regretful manner: *I must regretfully decline your invitation.* Regrettably means to be regretted: *Regrettably, all the casualties were caused by "friendly fire."*

Replace/substitute The distinction between these two words would not come to light so often were it not for the chronic illiteracy of sportscasters. If player A sprains his ankle and player B is called on to the field, player A has been replaced by player B, but player B has been substituted for player A. Commentators often say things like "Player A has been substituted by player B." Those sportscasters should be replaced.

Seasonable/seasonal Use seasonable to mean suitable to the circumstances or time of year, opportune: *It was a seasonable time of year to eat asparagus.* Use seasonal to mean to do with a particular time of year: *Strawberries are a seasonal fruit.*

Sensual/sensuous Sensual means pertaining to sexuality or the appetites of the flesh: *He was a libertine of gross sensuality.* Sensuous means satisfying to the senses: *The wind murmured sensuously in the trees.*

Situation A situation may be a place, a condition, or a even job. What it cannot be is a vague filler after another noun, or sometimes adjective, as in *no-win situation, a war situation, a crisis situation* or, worst of all, *an ongoing situation.*

Substantial This means having substance. The phrase "substantial damages" does not mean large damages, but damages of real value. The distinction is sometimes difficult to make, but is well illustrated in the term "a substantial citizen." Not a large citizen, but a citizen of substance, someone who is well off.

Tooth comb There is no such thing as a tooth comb. You may floss your teeth, but you do not comb them. The correct expression is a fine-tooth comb or a comb with small teeth. Such a comb would clearly comb very thoroughly; hence, the image of using a fine-tooth comb. All other variants—*fine tooth-comb, fine-tooth-comb*—are incorrect. Obviously incorrect. Manifest nonsense.

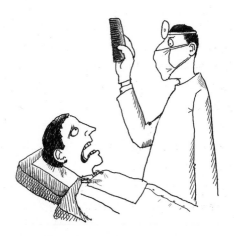

Unique An adjective that means being the only one of its kind. To use it to mean remarkable or outstanding is to waste its considerable force. In its pure meaning it cannot be modified. You cannot logically say very unique, quite unique, or absolutely unique. At a pinch you might say almost unique, but that is not the same thing as unique.

Very Weigh out all the very's in your writing and eliminate most. There are so many better alternatives!

These are the difficulties about "very":

- You should use it to modify only adjectives and adverbs. "Very good" and "very well" are correct, although one asks what "very" has added. "Very against" and, worse, "very into" are incorrect.

- You may use it with some verbs and verbal adjectives, but not with others. You can't say "very valued," but you can say "very depressed."

- Coupled with "real" it becomes gibberish. *I have very real doubts about this* is an inflated way of saying that you have doubts. And anyway, what are "slightly real" doubts?

- To use the word very is usually to concede that you have not chosen the right word in the first place. Very good? Excellent. Very small? Minute. Very intelligent? Brilliant.

Waive/wave To waive is to dispense with or to forgo: *Let us waive the formalities and use first names.* It can be confused with wave in its sense of dismiss: *He waved my objections aside.*

Afterword

The introduction to this book touched on the difficulty of deciding what is, and what is not, correct English. On the one hand, there are few hard rules, and when there are rules, there are many exceptions. As a result, both through inventiveness and casual use, the rules of language change all the time. Ultimately, usage is the arbiter of what words and constructions mean. On the other hand, any literate society needs a widely agreed body of vocabulary and grammar to communicate accurately, and agreement must take the form of rules.

If I have erred on the side of strictness, it is because the argument "usage decides all"—while an accurate *description* of how language works—is no use at all as a *prescription* of how to use it. For instance, the word *enormity* is so widely used to mean "excess of size" that usage certainly sanctions this meaning. But it retains its older meaning of "excess of wickedness," and if you boast about the "enormity" of your achievements, you can look foolish. So where the battle is not already hopelessly lost, I have dug in my heels and insisted—as I am sure your teachers did—that such and such a meaning is correct and other meanings incorrect. Each loss of precision diminishes the language's ability to make fine distinctions of meaning. It is a rear-guard action, but one well worth fighting.

There is another defense of strictness. Rules are made to be broken as well as observed, but you cannot break them effectively unless you know and understand them well. The best writers are able to create a style of such individuality and originality that they have no successful or unsuccessful imitators. Many do this by fooling around with the rules of English prose in distinctive ways.

If there seems to be a contradiction in this book between permissiveness on one hand and strictness on the other, it is because both attitudes are necessary if you are to express yourself vigorously, accurately, and colorfully in English.

Index

Further Reading

Bryson, Bill, *Mother Tongue: English and How It Got That Way*, Hamish Hamilton, 1990.

Fowler, H. W. and Fowler, F. G., *The King's English*, Oxford University Press, 1906; third edition with new introduction (Matthew Parris), OUP, 2002.

Fowler, H. W., *A Dictionary of Modern English Usage*, Oxford University Press, 1929; second edition, rev. Sir Ernest Gowers, OUP, 1965.

Gowers, Sir Ernest, *The Complete Plain Words*, HMSO 1948; second revised edition, ed. Sir Bruce Fraser, Penguin, 1970; third revised edition, ed. Sidney Greenbaum and Janet Whitcut, Penguin, 2004.

Hart, Horace H., *Hart's Rules for Compositors* and *Readers at the University Press*, Oxford, Oxford University Press, 1893; thirty-ninth edition 1983.

Parody, A., *Eats, Shites and Leaves: Crap English and How to Use It*, Michael O'Mara Books, 2004.

Partridge, Eric, *Usage and Abusage: A Modern Guide to Good English*, Hamish Hamilton, 1942; third revised edition, Penguin, 2005.

Taggart, Caroline and Wines, J. A., *My Grammar and I (or should that be 'Me'?): old-school ways to sharpen your english*, Michael O'Mara Books, 2008.

Trask, R. L., *Mind the Gaffe: The Penguin Guide to Common Errors in English*, Penguin, 2002.

Trask, R. L., *The Penguin Dictionary of English Grammar*, Penguin, 2000.

Weiner, E. S. C. and Delahunty, Andrew (eds), *The Oxford Guide to English Usage: The essential guide to correct English*, second revised edition, Oxford University Press, 1994.

ENJOY THESE OTHER
READER'S DIGEST BESTSELLERS

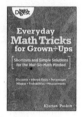

Everyday Math Tricks for Grown-Ups

Lively text and simple examples illustrate all the basics—addition, subtraction, multiplication, and division—with easy-to-remember ways to deal with all of the math challenges you face each and every day.

Kjartan Poskitt
978-1-60652-329-2
$9.95 paperback

I Used to Know That

Make learning fun again with these lighthearted pages that are packed with important theories, phrases, and those long-forgotten "rules" you once learned in school.

Caroline Taggart
ISBN 978-0-7621-0995-1
$14.95 hardcover

My Grammar and I...
Or Should That Be Me?

Confused about when to use "its" or "it's" or the correct spelling of "principal" or "principle"? Avoid language pitfalls and let this entertaining and practical guide improve both your speaking and writing skills.

Caroline Taggart
J. A. Wines
ISBN 978-1-60652-026-0
$14.95 hardcover

For more information, visit us at RDTradePublishing.com
E-book editions also available.

Reader's Digest books can be purchased through retail and online bookstores.
In the United States books are distributed by Penguin Group (USA), Inc.
For more information or to order books, call 1-800-788-6262.